Table of Contents

INTRODUCTION	1
NAVIGATION PAGE	3
PASSIVE INCOME FOR LIFE	5
PREFACE	7
ABOUT THE AUTHOR	10
WHY YOU NEED THIS BOOK	11
EVEN THE GREAT PYRAMID STARTED BY LAYING THE FIRST BLOCK	14
AMAZON SELLING BASICS	16
OK… NOW, HOW DO I FIGURE OUT WHAT TO SELL?	20
HOW I STARTED BUILDING MY AMAZON EMPIRE… FOR CHEAP	22
MY FIRST YEAR OF AMAZON SELLING: SUCCESSES AND LESSONS LEARNED	26
BREAKING IT DOWN: CATEGORIES OF USED ITEMS TO SELL	35
INCREASE PROFITS AND SELL ITEMS FASTER BY MAKING BETTER ITEM DESCRIPTIONS ON AMAZON	43
PRICING AND INVENTORY MANAGEMENT PRACTICES THAT YIELD MORE AMAZON SALES	47
CUSTOMER RELATIONS PRACTICES AND MAINTAINING A HIGH CUSTOMER FEEDBACK PERCENTAGE	52
DIVERSIFYING YOUR AMAZON BUSINESS: SELLING PRODUCTS ON CRAIGSLIST, EBAY AND ETSY	57
ADDITIONAL LINKS FOR FURTHER RESEARCH	60
THANK YOU, READERS!	65
ALMOST FREE MONEY	67
PREFACE	69
ABOUT THE AUTHOR	72
START-UP: INITIAL ASSESSMENT	74
HOW AND WHERE TO SELL	77
SELLING ON EBAY AND AMAZON	79
WHERE TO FIND ITEMS TO SELL	85

FINDING INVENTORY ONLINE	90
THE BOTTOM LINE ON EBAY BUYING	94
GARAGE SALES SHOPPING	96
RESEARCHING	100
FREE ITEMS TO SELL: OUTDOORS	104
ORGANIC ITEMS	106
MAN-MADE ITEMS	108
SELLING SCRAP METAL: EASIEST MONEY YOU'LL EVER MAKE	112
GETTING STARTED SELLING SCRAP METAL	114
A TRIP TO THE SCRAP METAL DEALER	118
PRECIOUS METALS: FAST, EASY MONEY	122
WHERE TO FIND GOLD FOR CHEAP	128
WHAT TO DO WITH YOUR GOLD AND SILVER CONTACTS	132
NOTES ON PRECIOUS METALS IN COINS!	134
NOTES ON SATELLITE DISHES AND RECEIVERS	136
SELLING SCRAP METAL ON EBAY	138
TO KEEP ASSEMBLED, OR DISASSEMBLE; THAT IS THE QUESTION!	141
MAXIMIZE PROFITS IN VINTAGE ELECTRONICS	145
TREATING YOUR BUSINESS AS A BUSINESS: INCOME TAX ISSUES	151
DONATIONS	154
THANK YOU, READERS!	155
WEBSITES AND LINKS	157
RECOMMENDED PAY SITES:	161
GARAGE SALE SUPERSTAR	**199**
INTRODUCTION	201
GENERAL INFORMATION	203
GARAGE SALE AND YARD SALE TIPS	204
GARAGE SALE ORGANIZATION	206
GARAGE SALE ADVERTISING	210
GARAGE SALE DAYS OF THE WEEK	213
GARAGE SALE START TIME AND HOURS	215
WHEN TO START YOUR GARAGE SALE	216
GARAGE SALE SIGNS AND STICKERS	218
SIGN SIZE AND DESIGN	219
SIGN CONSTRUCTION	221
GARAGE SALE STICKERS	223
GARAGE SALE PRICING	225

GARAGE SALE PRICING GUIDE	226
AFTER YOUR GARAGE SALE: GETTING RID OF YOUR STUFF FOR FREE	233
YARD SALE TIPS	235
CONCLUSION	237
WEBSITES AND LINKS	238

INTRODUCTION

In our current economic condition, everybody is looking for new ways to make some extra money for themselves and their family. What if I told you that there was a way to spend your pocket change and earn consistent returns of 500% profit?

You would probably say: "Yeah, right. Nobody can turn that kind of profit."

Well, I will tell you what. I have been doing just that for over fourteen years, and so can you. The Almost Free Money and Passive Income for Life systems can be applied anywhere in the world and you need almost zero start-up cash.

If you can turn on a computer and take a photograph with a digital camera or cell phone, you can make the same income that I have. The best part of this business model is: Once you list the items into your business inventory, 90% of your work is done. You just ship sold items and collect your money!

If you are already a fan of the Almost Free Money books, a lot has happened since the title book of the series was released less than two years ago. The Almost Free Money books have sold thousands of copies in both digital form on Amazon Kindle and in softcover book form on

Amazon. Three of the books have been #1 Amazon bestsellers in their categories. Passive Income for Life was #1 overall in the home business category for two months.

Two blogs have been launched: http://www.EricMichaelBooks.com now hosts some over 80 outstanding discussions on flipping used items, thrift shopping, finding gold, selling scrap metal, selling vintage collectibles and selling items on eBay, Amazon and Etsy.com. http://www.garagesaleacademy.com is now one of the highest traffic websites on the internet for garage sale hosts and garage sale shoppers.

In this value pack of Almost Free Money books, you receive three full-length books from the Almost Free Money series, and they are the top selling and top rated volumes of the series:

Almost Free Money: Learn how to find items for free or under $1 in a multitude of locations, including your own home, while recreating, scrap metal and second-hand shopping and then sell them for large profits on the internet from home.

Passive Income for Life: Develop your own passive income and/or supplementary income by building a high-yielding Amazon income for very low costs.

Garage Sale Superstar: Learn how to maximize your garage sale or yard sale to yield maximum profit. Learn vital garage sale organization, advertising, pricing and customer relations strategies from veterans of thousands of garage sales.

While you are reading the books, please keep in mind that you can really help me out by leaving a positive (5-Star reviews are awesome!) by clicking on: http://www.amazon.com/dp/B00HUCT90S. Thank you.

NAVIGATION PAGE

BOOK ONE: PASSIVE INCOME FOR LIFE   4

BOOK TWO: ALMOST FREE MONEY

BOOK THREE: GARAGE SALE SUPERSTAR

PASSIVE INCOME FOR LIFE

A Time-Tested Secret Recipe for Building a $50,000 Cash Machine on Amazon.com...In Your Spare Time

PREFACE

In this book, we are going to start right off flying. We are going to get excited about the opportunity to set up a long term investment for you and your family that will pay you consistently and constantly for many years to come for the work that you are going to do in the next several months.

I know what you are thinking. Who is *this* guy, and why should I drink *his* Kool-Aid? This seems too good to be true.

Who am I? I am just like you. I am just an average guy who was looking for a second income to help with paying the bills. I did a lot of research on the internet regarding passive income and building a home business on the internet. Then, I just started building assets.

With only the help of my wife and spending less than $20 a week and in some cases only spending my own pocket change, I built an inventory on the largest retail site in the world that is worth well over $50,000. I built this inventory in only two years, while working a demanding full-time job, and while dividing my "spare" time with my two young children. Yes, I still made it to every baseball game that they played, went camping, and made regular trips to the beach.

Now, after five years of managing my Amazon business, my family's groceries are paid for every week by Amazon, and we bought presents for our entire Christmas list thanks to Amazon customer orders placed during one week in December!

My wife and I now spend about two hours a week on our Amazon business packaging and shipping sold items to customers, and even *that* two hours can be eliminated by opting in to Amazon's Fulfillment by Amazon (FBA) program.

I enjoyed the process of building our Amazon inventory. It was not like "work" at all. And, the best thing about Amazon (eBay sellers, take notice!) is that it is FREE, FREE, FREE to list items into your inventory. That's right. You pay nothing to build your inventory, besides the small cost of the items themselves.

In this book, I will teach you how I have found hundreds of items for FREE that I subsequently listed on Amazon for an *average* of $8.50 per item. I have also sold many free items for over $25 each, and several individual items for over $50.

You will also learn how to routinely find items for under $1, and sell them on Amazon for well over five times the value on average. Of our 8,200 current inventory items, I would estimate that well over 7500 were found and bought for under $1. Many items were purchased for 10 cents or 25 cents each.

The point that I am trying to make, as we get to know each other, is this: I have built a nice passive income for my family with very little initial cost *and* with no prior selling experience. I learned everything myself, and it was very easy to accomplish. I can show you exactly what I did to build my business, and then *you can do it, too.*

This process will work well for anybody, regardless of your location (in the civilized world), age, sex, physical disabilities, or computer skills. You CAN do the same thing that I did and build a large productive Amazon inventory in less than two years.

I will tell you exactly what I did to build our Amazon business, show you how to find the best items to sell, and teach you how to use the internet to research new sources for your inventory. Here is the bottom line... if you read this book and follow the instructions provided, you *will* make money. Easy money. Free money, in some cases.

But, you will have to work, and spend some time on your new business. So, let's get right to it!

ABOUT THE AUTHOR

Eric Michael is married and is a proud father of two energetic sons. He enjoys family outings and many outdoor activities, including fishing, hunting and camping.

The information provided in this book and in the Almost Free Money series was compiled during twelve years of internet research and his personal experiences have developed a unique skill set – the ability to find a diverse selection of free items (or priced under $1) that could be sold on the internet for surprisingly good profit.

He has gone on to develop a popular website titled Garage Sale Academy, which incorporates portions of the Almost Free Money series, and expands into other arenas of profiting from flipping garage sale, thrift store and flea market finds, as well as helping garage sale hosts make maximum profits from their garage sales.

He also hosts Facebook fan pages for Almost Free Money and Garage Sale Academy, as well as a Garage Sale Blog and Forum.

WHY YOU NEED THIS BOOK

I am excited to share my story with you and get you out there looking for inventory, so you can start making some money. But first, we need to lay out the game plan for this book and discuss reader expectations for the topics that will be covered here.

What you will get from this book:

1. In this book, we are going to start from scratch and build a large Amazon inventory that earns you a significant e-check that goes into your bank account every two weeks (or more often, if you prefer).

2. We will go through the basics of selling on Amazon. Even if you have never been on Amazon's website, you will be able to start selling on Amazon. You will know how to list inventory items and process orders (oh... and collect your money from Amazon, too!)

3. I will teach you everything that you need to know to research which types of inventory items to sell. You can figure out for yourself which road is right for you. You should sell in categories that you are familiar with and/or enjoy working in.

4. I will tell you exactly what I have sold on Amazon and why those items worked for me. My 'per-item cost' was only 8 cents an item, the last time that I calculated it. My average sales price was just over $8.50 per item.

5. We will discuss managing your inventory and effective pricing of inventory items, so that your inventory sells quickly and you have more money to increase the size of your inventory.

6. As we proceed through this book, I will provide you with some resources that will help you to build your background knowledge, learn Amazon selling techniques, and find new categories of inventory items in which to sell.

7. You have already been provided with my contact information in the 'About the Author' chapter. Readers are encouraged to stop by and chat or ask questions. We have over 3,000 contacts on Facebook and Twitter for you to network with and bounce ideas off of. We love hearing from fellow Amazon selling friends through Facebook, Twitter and on Garage Sale Academy's Facebook links. Stop by and say hello, as you progress through this book. Provide an introduction, and then tell everybody how your business has grown!

What you will NOT get from this book:

1. A get-rich-quick plan. Although I started selling items within several days of finding my first inventory item, it does take considerable time and effort to build an Amazon inventory that provides a regular and significant passive income. You will also have to re-build your inventory as your items sell. This is a home business, and you will have to work at it to be successful. After reading this book, you will have the advantage of hearing what worked for me, but you will still have to apply the knowledge that you learned and work as hard as I did to build a comparable inventory. Nothing is given to you in this world. If you are not willing to work, do not read any further.

2. This is not an Amazon selling primer. We will cover everything you need to know to build your inventory and maintain your business effectively. But, Amazon does an excellent job of providing Amazon sellers all of the background information that they need to run their business on a day-to-day level. Their Seller Help pages are very easy to understand and navigate. There is also a ton of information online and in other Kindle books for beginning sellers, so this book will not cover that subject in detail.

3. Thanks again to the loyal readers of the Almost Free Money series. I just wanted to take a second to let you know that it was necessary to lay down some basics for readers who have not read Almost Free Money or Fast Cash. If you have read either of these books, some of the introductory topics in this book may seem a bit familiar to you. Everything else in this book is fresh information. It is not recycled contents from our other books or Garage Sale Academy webpages.

There. Now we have laid the guidelines for this book. Now let's get the basics out of the way, so we can get to the fun stuff – shopping for great items to put in your Amazon inventory!

Chapter Summary:

Benefits of reading this book:

1. Build a passive income that generates consistent and profitable paychecks
2. Learn Amazon selling basics. Start listing items immediately.
3. How I buy low and sell high on Amazon
4. How to build your Amazon business and manage your inventory for maximum sales
5. Learn how to research new income sources
6. Links to vital how-to pages on the internet
7. Where to network with other sellers – Social Media connections

What this site is Not:

1. An Amazon selling instructional book
2. A get-rich-quick book

EVEN THE GREAT PYRAMID STARTED BY LAYING THE FIRST BLOCK

The title says it all. If you want to be able to build your pyramid to the very top block hundreds of feet above the other Amazon businesses out there, you need to build a wide and sturdy base for your Amazon pyramid.

The ancient Egyptians did not start building pyramids without developing a plan first, right? Don't you think that they had to figure out how wide to make the structure and how big the blocks would have to be before they started making their slaves move those thousand pound blocks around?

The same principles apply to your Amazon business. Before you start building your pyramid, you have to draw up your blueprint. You must know several things before you start buying inventory for your business.

1. Inventory storage – The amount of space that you have to store your inventory often dictates the types of items that you will buy for your inventory. If you live in an apartment, you will be limited to selling items that do not take up a lot of room, such as media items. You will be looking for items like CDs and books that can be shelved or placed in boxes while they are in your inventory.

We are lucky. We have a good portion of our finished basement in which to store inventory items. We have a 20 x 6' area that houses our music inventory shelves, seven cupboards full of collectibles, board games, and shipping supplies, and also a utility room that is used for storing large inventory items.

2. What types of items do you want to sell? Before you start shopping for inventory items, it is important to know what your main source of income is going to be. This should be determined by your background knowledge (which can be enhanced through research) and your enthusiasm for the topic. In my experience, Amazon sellers do MUCH better when they have a passion for the items that they are selling to their customers. These sellers find better products, describe the items more accurately in item descriptions, and take more care in shipping the sold items to customers. This all adds up to receiving better customer reviews and getting more return customers – two of an Amazon seller's best friends!

Chapter Summary:

What to do before you start buying inventory:

1. Determine how much room that you have for inventory storage
2. Decide which types of items that you are interested in selling

AMAZON SELLING BASICS

If you asked ten random people on the street how they would go about selling a used item, at least seven of them would probably answer: 1) a garage sale or 2) eBay. One of them might say Craigslist.

Very few people know that you can sell used items on Amazon. Many experienced internet sellers do not even know how easy and profitable it is to sell used items on Amazon. Most of your competition is trying to sell used items via eBay auctions, and that market is not as profitable as it used to be. The auction format has lost its appeal to many consumers. Today, many consumers want to locate the item that they want to buy and purchase it immediately rather than place bids and wait a week to see if they won an auction.

EBay does offer fixed price items, but the largest and most recognized internet marketplace is Amazon.com, and it is not even a close competition. The great thing about the way Amazon is set up is that each item offers several different condition ratings for each item. If you have a used book or CD to sell, it will be listed on the same page as new books from the manufacturer in that particular title.

Why is that such a big deal? Many consumers today are looking for the best possible deal available to them. Often they will browse items with the intent of buying a new item. However, when consumers navigate to the item description page, and see that your CD which is listed as 'Used - Like New' costs about half the price of a brand new item, they may opt to buy your used CD over the pricier new CD listing.

Keep in mind that it is very possible to regularly find used CDs at yard sales for 25 cents, or even for free, as we will discuss later. Amazon provides even inexperienced sellers the opportunity to consistently sell many different types of items at large profit margins. This is what we will be focusing on in this book. But first, we have to learn how to sell items on Amazon.

The first thing that you will have to do is sign up for an Amazon seller account. The process is self-explanatory. Go to the [Amazon seller webpage](), and fill in the required information. You will be providing Amazon your financial information for a checking or saving account, which your earning disbursements will be deposited into on a regular basis. The process is secure. You do not need to worry about providing your information over the internet, if you have not done so before. Amazon is a huge corporation with thousands of individual seller accounts, and they take their information security very seriously.

You will be provided two options from which you must select the type of Amazon seller account that you want to have – Basic or Pro Merchant.

By default, you start with a Basic selling account. With the basic selling account, you can list inventory items for free. When your item sells, Amazon credits your account with the amount that you chose to price your item at, minus several fees.

If you sold a book priced at $10 from your basic selling account, you would be charged an 8-20% Amazon finder's fee, a closing fee of about $1.35, and a 99 cent per-item fee. You are then credited with a shipping credit, which varies by item type. This shipping credit often results in the closing fee being covered, as you are given a $3.99 shipping credit for books, for example. Most books cost under $3 to actually ship via USPS.

Once you build a medium sized inventory and you believe that you will be regularly selling at least forty items a month (this will not take you long), you should opt out of the basic selling account and upgrade to the Pro Merchant selling account.

The Pro Merchant account has several major perks. First, the 99 cent per-item fee is waived for all items sold. Second, Pro Merchants have the ability to make their own item description pages and add them to the Amazon marketplace. I use this functionality quite often for rare high-end collectibles. The Pro Merchant account is currently $39.99, and the fee is deducted from your selling account profits. So, you do not have to pay a separate fee by credit card. It is deducted from your Amazon earnings account on a monthly basis.

After you have signed up for your account, there is a collection of helpful pages for new Amazon sellers at the [Amazon Help Pages](#).

You will want to spend some time here, and perhaps print off some pages and make some notes. If you start to feel a little nervous about the processes... DON'T worry! Selling on Amazon is incredibly easy. It is much simpler than selling an item on eBay and twice as fast, once you have gone through the process a couple of times.

Here is the complete process of selling a used item on Amazon:

1) Find the UPC or ISBN number on the bar code of the item that you want to sell. You can also type in the item's text title or description in the search bar.

2) Go to the Amazon home page. Type the UPC or ISBN number into the search bar at the top of the page. Find the item description page for the item that you want to list. In other words, if you are attempting to list a used copy of the CD 'Pearl Jam – 10', find Pearl Jam 10 in the Amazon search results. Click on the link. You will see a page that gives customers the details of the songs on the CD, along with multiple price listings from other Amazon sellers who are trying to sell Pearl Jam 10.

3) On the top right-hand corner of the description page in a dark blue box, you will see 'Do You Have One to Sell? Sell Yours Here' Click there.

4) Provide the condition and a short description of your item, list your price, and make it available for sale. Congratulations! Your item is now listed on Amazon and in your seller inventory. It took you about 30 seconds to list it, right? Welcome to the power of Amazon.

5) When your item sells on Amazon, you are sent a notice to your registered email address notifying you of the sale, and the customer details, along with the shipping method that they selected.

6) On your Amazon Seller Account page, you will see the sold item(s) listed there. You are provided a link to 'Buy Shipping' for that order. You complete the information for the shipping label, and print out the label with a standard printer. Tape the label on the box and ship it. Bam! Item out, money in your account. Done.

Chapter Summary:

- Amazon has little competition for many used items
- Why used items sell from new item pages
- Links to Amazon Help pages

How to start selling on Amazon:

1. Sign up for Amazon selling account
2. Basic vs. Pro Merchant Accounts
3. Explanation of Amazon fees
4. Step by step process for listing an inventory item on Amazon

OK... NOW, HOW DO I FIGURE OUT WHAT TO SELL?

The most important thing that an Amazon seller can do to increase earnings and profit margins earned on inventory items sold is to learn how to research. The learning process should be a continuous effort. Learning about new sources of inventory and methods for improving business procedures should not wane after you become an experienced seller.

The Amazon landscape is always evolving. Technology makes used items obsolete or undesirable. Consumer appetites change and the demand for pop culture media items can decline rapidly. Sellers have to be able to adjust to these changes accordingly. This is where research is vital. As a seller, you have to know what consumers are buying and how much they are willing to pay for items.

There are a variety of places that can help you to determine what types of items are hot, and what other sellers are doing well with.

Social media is probably the easiest way to research current trends. There is a lot of information in Facebook and Twitter. There are groups dedicated to talking about selling on Amazon, and also the eBay Underground Facebook group has a category about selling on Amazon that has active discussions.

Conduct a simple search on Google or Bing search engines for 'sell used items on Amazon tips', or a similar search query and you will have dozens of free sources of information. There are also many Kindle books devoted to the topic.

You can also read about the sub-topic that you are interested in. For instance, Weber's Barcode Booty is an informative book about selling used media and books on Amazon. Most of the books on Kindle are affordable – many books are priced between $3 and $10. Quite often, you can also find good Amazon books on 'Free Book Promotions'.

Our website Garage Sale Academy.com also has many pages that can assist sellers with finding inventory and also learning how to improve listings and develop good business practices. Among the topics with devoted webpages: How to sell on Amazon, Amazon packaging and shipping, how to sell used books, CDs, DVDs, video games, collectibles and used clothes, how to sell Amazon textbooks, how to find the best items at garage sales, thrift stores, and flea markets. There are also many links provided that direct readers to the best free niche sites related to selling used items.

Chapter Summary:

- The value and importance of research
- Demand for Amazon items changes frequently

Where to start researching types of used items to sell

1. Internet searches and search engine queries
2. Social Media
3. Kindle Books
4. Garage Sale Academy

HOW I STARTED BUILDING MY AMAZON EMPIRE... FOR CHEAP

I started selling used items for profit about twelve years ago. At that time, there was significantly less competition. It was easy to find treasure at garage sales and sell the items on eBay for excellent profit margins.

For the first five years of my business, I sold primarily used collectibles and media items on eBay, and I did well. Over time, several things happened. #1, I got tired of spending all of my time making eBay auctions, and #2, profit margins on eBay shrank as more and more internet sellers discovered how easy it was to sell used items and collectibles on eBay.

It became harder and harder to find quality collectibles at second-hand locations and eBay was getting tougher to sell effectively. Besides that, eBay continually increased their selling fees and changed their customer feedback structure so that it made it very hard to keep your seller feedback rating high unless you were a high volume seller.

Many collectible item auctions were also ending without a bid. I got tired of paying eBay listing fees, and getting little in return, in many cases. So, I started looking for other ways to diversify my used item sales. Almost immediately, I discovered selling used items on Amazon.

When I first started selling on Amazon, very few sellers sold used items there. As a matter of fact, very few internet sellers even knew that it was possible to sell used items on Amazon.

Heck yeah, I thought. Amazon is a huge marketplace, with less competition than on eBay, and you don't even have to pay listing fees (as on eBay). Let's do this!

My only concern at the time was trying to decide if my efforts would be worthwhile, because I did not know if there would be sufficient demand on Amazon for the used items that I was finding at garage sales, thrift stores, and other second-hand locations.

I started by doing a lot of browsing on the Amazon marketplace.

If you are new to selling on Amazon, it is vital for you to do the same thing that I did. How does spending hours surfing on Amazon help you to sell more items? You get an excellent feel for which categories of items you can make high profit margins in. You learn which types of used items can be sold effectively on Amazon.

I looked at many, many categories of items, and I looked at a lot of individual item pages. I took notes on which categories had used items that were highly priced, and which categories were flooded with used items and therefore not worth my time.

I also noted which types of used items sold very slowly on Amazon. One very helpful feature that you can use to gauge the popularity of items and determine how quickly you can expect to make a sale is the Amazon 'Best Seller's Rank' on each item's description page. This ranking is displayed about halfway down the item page. You will find ranks of anywhere from single digits down to over one million for some rare books. The lower the best seller rank is, the faster the item will typically sell.

How are ranks used to decide what types of items to buy? They provide you with an idea of how long you can expect items to stay on your inventory shelves before you sell them.

Nothing is written in stone. You may find a very rare book that has a Best Sellers Rank of 320,000 and have a collector buy it the same day. It is also more likely that the book will go unsold for at least several months. Or, it may never sell at all.

Should you buy the book with the rank of 320K? It depends on several things.

If you can buy the book for $1, and you know that the lowest Amazon price listed by other sellers is $80, then obviously it would be worth it to buy the book and list it into your inventory. For that profit margin, I would let that book sit on my shelf for years!

I prefer to have a range of best seller ranks in my inventory.. I like to have some items that sell fairly quickly (low best seller rank numbers), so I have liquid funds that I can use to buy more inventory items.

It is also perfectly acceptable to me to have a fairly high percentage of my items ranked in the tens of thousands or higher, as long as the list price is high. Those $80-100 sales of rare items that occur periodically are nice chunks of change, and you WILL find these rare items regularly at second-hand locations, once you know what to look for.

Of course, the amount of slow sellers that you will be buying will depend on how much storage room you have for your inventory. If you do not have much shelving, you may not be able to buy as many large items or rare items that will probably take months to sell. You will have to buy more quick sellers that get sold regularly and get shipped out, which makes room in your inventory for new arrivals.

When I was researching how to start selling used items on Amazon, I also read all of the Frequently Asked Questions for New Amazon Sellers, and I became familiar with the listing and shipping procedures. I read most of the Help pages, so I knew what I was doing BEFORE I started listing items into my inventory.

Once I was done with that, I started figuring out which types of items I would be looking to buy at second-hand locations and then sell on Amazon.

I was amazed at how many types of used items could be sold on Amazon. Media items like books and music have always been Amazon's bread-and-butter. Used media items are easy to find for cheap and they do very well. However, I learned that I could also sell used toys, games, electronics, components, rechargeable batteries, housewares, holiday décor, and much more! In fact, most of these used items were selling for significantly higher prices on Amazon than on eBay, and not many existing Amazon sellers were selling used items in these categories.

Even today, although the amount of used item sellers on Amazon has increased, many individual item pages still have very few used listings. Quite often, I am the only seller with a used item listing. This is great, because I get to set the market when I list my used item's price.

Because I had already been selling used items on eBay for five years or so, I knew the types of used items that I routinely found at garage sales and thrift stores, and the price I could typically buy them for. Now, after doing my research, I had a good idea of which types of used items I could sell on Amazon, how long they would take to sell on average, and the profit margin that they would yield when they sold.

My forte has always been finding used items for under $1 and selling them for high profit margins. Initially, I built a very nice inventory of used and collectible books. 95% of these books I bought for 25 to 50 cents at garage sales. Many of these books I actually found in Free Boxes. More details about finding high value Amazon items for free can be found on our website, on a dedicated webpage.

I sold a lot of these 25 cent books for $20-50. We will talk about how to maximize your return on specific types of items later in this book.

Chapter Summary:

How I started building my $50,000 Amazon business

- Prior experience selling on other sites
- How I found Amazon
- What types of used items to sell on Amazon
- Read the Amazon Help pages for sellers

MY FIRST YEAR OF AMAZON SELLING: SUCCESSES AND LESSONS LEARNED

The most important thing for an Amazon seller to do is to BUILD UP AN INVENTORY. It is important to be patient. You WILL sell some items for good profits in your first several months of Amazon selling, but it is more important to get a supply of high-yielding items into your inventory. These will often take some time to sell.

Remember, as you add more items to your inventory, you are building your business. Your business will provide you a nice passive income for years. Once you build a large Amazon inventory, your used item business will make money every day. You will even make money while you sleep and while you are on vacation! Awesome, right?!

In my first year of building my Amazon business, I concentrated on keeping expenditures very low. I bought a <u>bunch</u> of books and CD's for 25 cents and under at yard sales. I also got a lot of books for free from family, friends, my home, and at garage sales in free boxes.

One thing that worked in my favor was that the used items that sold the best on Amazon were very easy to find. I spent at most ten hours a week locating inventory items and another couple of hours listing items on Amazon. Usually, I hit garage sales and yard sales on Friday and Saturday mornings. When I started, almost all of my Amazon inventory items were found at garage sales. Most of these items were ten cents or a quarter.

Usually, I tried to visit at least twenty garage sales a weekend. I put all of my items that I found in boxes, and then listed them on Amazon later in the week while I watched TV. How's that for a tough job, eh? Going to garage sales and making money while you watch TV – still sounds pretty good to me, even after ten years in this business.

Keep in mind that this was before the days of Smart Phones and Price Checker apps. It was fun listing the items that I had found to see how much profit I was going to make on each one when it sold on Amazon. Almost every weekend, I would find several books worth at least $50. I would also have to discard some books because they were "penny books" on Amazon, due to oversaturation of that title on the Amazon marketplace. I collected all of my penny books, and then I either listed them as large lots of books on eBay for $10, or took them to Goodwill for a tax write-off.

After several weeks of building my Amazon inventory, I had already outgrown my two large bookshelves that I had initially dedicated to housing my Amazon books.

So, that brings us to the first and most important thing that I learned during my first month of Amazon selling: **You HAVE to have an inventory management system**. It saves you a ton of time if you know exactly where your inventory items are, so that when your item sells, you can immediately find your item for shipping.

If I knew then what I know now, I would have developed my system before I started buying inventory, and I would have set up my storage area to allow for a much larger inventory. The more room that you have for your business' inventory to expand, the less hassle you will have down the road.

It would have saved me a lot of wasted time and shuffling items around full bookshelves, which is a real chore. I had to add buy and add bookshelves several different times in the first couple of months. Then, I had to move books around a lot to get them to fit on my existing shelves.

I spent too much time organizing, when I could have been out buying more inventory items. That was part of my learning process.

Take my word for it. Find a way to dedicate a fairly good sized storage area to your Amazon inventory, and make sure that you have at least five large shelving units and/or cupboards to store items in. You will fill them up quickly.

I started with two 5' tall bookshelves, and I easily filled them within a month. Now, our inventory consists of ten 5' x 3' shelves, four large cupboards, and another storage area full of inventory items, and we have downsized recently.

Many Amazon sellers mark their shelves or storage units with a designated number or letter combination, and then note that number in each Amazon listing, so that they can quickly find the item when it sells.

Anything that can save you minutes or even seconds each time you process an Amazon sale should be strongly considered. Keep in mind that over the course of your business, you will probably process tens of thousands of orders. This time you have saved by organizing properly adds up quickly, and the time you save can be spent doing other things, like enjoying time with your family.

When you are setting up your storage and packaging areas, consider organizing them so that you eliminate as much wasted time as possible. Keep your storage and packing areas as close together as possible. Make sure that you can find inventory items immediately, without having to search through multiple shelves. Ensure that storage areas are well-lit so that you can see the titles of your media items. Keep your packing area organized, so that you know where to find the correct sized boxes for packaging items for shipment.

Another concept that helped me out a lot in my first year of Amazon selling was to **start selling what I already knew about and enjoyed looking for**. Because I had already been selling books on eBay for five years, the transition to Amazon was as smooth as silk. I already knew which books were worth buying at garage sales, how to describe books and their specific condition issues, and how to store and ship books.

By selling types of items that you are familiar with, you lower the learning curve and increase the probability of finding valuable items. It also helps a great deal to enjoy what you sell. I know… that sounds like it should be common sense, but there are many internet sellers who choose their genres based only on profit. These types of sellers often burn out quickly or bounce around from genre to genre, never mastering any single category of items.

But, I digress. Let's get back to the story line. By the end of the first month or so, I had filled about two and a half 5 x 3' shelves with books. My Amazon inventory contained about 850 books and I had only spent about $30 of my money and spent about 50 hours of my spare time to get the inventory listed and shelved.

My average list price during my first month was between $4-5. If you figure that the average price spent to buy that inventory was only about 6 cents an item, the profit margin was still excellent. During that first month, I listed a lot of my own books on Amazon, and I got quite a few more of my family's excess books for free. That was why the cost was only 6 cents per item.

After the first month of selling used books on Amazon, sales fluctuated from week to week. The first week I sold a couple of books, and then I sold nothing during week two. The third week, I believe I sold at least ten books, and that was when I started selling a couple of higher value books ($40-50), as well.

The point that I am trying to make is that it takes a while to start making profit. Do not expect to start selling items immediately, unless you choose a category that has a high demand, such as newer video games (which will cost you significantly more money to build your inventory).

In most cases, the number of sales and also the consistency of your sales will mirror your inventory numbers. You will not start seeing a constant flow of sales until you build your inventory to a sufficient level, and that level is determined by your choice(s) of inventory items.

For me, it took about three months of steady building to an inventory of about 2,000 items before sales really started to roll in consistently. It was also nice to hit that inventory level because items were starting to move off of my shelves faster as they sold on Amazon.

By then, I was getting a lot better at picking "winners". My per-item average rose significantly (probably doubled) by the third month. So, as some of the books I had listed in the first couple of weeks were finally selling and getting shipped out, I was able to replace them with higher value books, which raised the average list price. Woo hoo!

From about the third month on, I knew that I could make consistent money selling used items on Amazon. I started to look for ways to diversify my inventory. We will discuss the pros and cons of diversification in a later chapter, but suffice it to say, I don't like having all of my eggs in one basket. That was one of the reasons I started researching other sources of cheap inventory for my Amazon business.

Having a number of different things to look for while I was "picking" also made looking for inventory at yard sales more fun. I started adding items like: CDs, video games, board games and used toys.

At about that same time, I shifted from picking primarily at garage sales to spending a significant amount of time at thrift stores and second-hand stores. Thrift stores are akin to visiting one hundred garage sales, all under one roof!

I saved a lot of gas money by only driving to one or two locations, instead of forty. The condition of the items is also much better at thrift stores, as employees only place items of at least a decent quality on their shelves. The other donated junk (which you often see at yard sales) gets tossed in the dumpster.

Thrift stores provide the opportunity to find some excellent high-value items, especially in areas where there is not an overabundance of Amazon sellers. Some items have a lot of competition in most thrift stores (books, for instance). But, if you do your research on diversifying types of inventory items, you will have a leg up on 90% of the other sellers who focus only on the easy items, like books.

Thrift stores also require a bit more experience and patience than garage sales. At garage sales, many items are underpriced. At thrift stores, the used items usually cost more to buy, so you have to be careful that you can make a minimum profit on each item.

It is easy to lose money on items bought at thrift stores. It did not take me many visits to the local thrift shop to figure out that I had better be careful buying hardcover books for $2! I was finding several $20 hardcover books, but I was also taking some hits on some penny books. Again, this was before the advent of the Smart phone, which now allows you to check current Amazon prices using a bar code scanner and/or photograph of the book that you are considering for purchase.

Thrift stores are also time savers. If you have limited time, you can pick dozens of items at a thrift store in under an hour. Thrifts also provide you the opportunity to shop during the week and after work. Garage sales limit you to picking on the weekends, when often, you would rather be doing other recreational activities with your family or friends.

During the fourth or fifth month of Amazon selling, I also started looking for large lots of items to break up and sell as single items on Amazon. I found a lot of good deals on eBay on large boxes of books. It was common to find 25-50 item lots of books on eBay five years ago for cheap. At that time, there were a lot of eBay sellers who only sold books on that website and not on Amazon.

I routinely found valuable book titles in those large lots that paid for the entire lot all by themselves. All of the other books were gravy. It was obvious that the seller had tried to list all of the books on eBay, and then threw them all into a lot after they did not get a bid on eBay. Many rare books do not get bid within one week on an eBay auction because few eBay bidders are looking for their particular subject. The eBay seller's loss is the Amazon seller's gain.

I found a lot of $20-30 books buried in $5 eBay book lot auctions. Even after paying for the shipping fees, I often listed over $100 worth of profit. Obviously, not every lot was a winner, but I won much more than I broke even. I also won a lot of single book auctions at the minimum bid of $1, and then listed the same book on Amazon for over $20.

Many of the auctions that I was bidding on had misspelled titles, were listed in the wrong category, or had very poor item descriptions and photographs. In some cases, I even flipped the same book back onto eBay with a good description and multiple photos, and turned some quick and significant profits.

I also finally "went big" during the fifth month. I found a deal that I couldn't pass up, while I was searching through bulk book lots on eBay. An eBay seller had listed about a thousand books that did not sell at her garage sale. The eBay auction only had a couple of minutes left and had not received a bid for $50.

My initial thought was… 'My wife would kill me. Where would we put 1,000 more books?!'

I decided to take a risk. At a penny or two a book, how could I lose, right?

To make a long story short, I won the auction for $50, and had to drive for three hours and pick up about 1200 pounds of books in our lightweight S.U.V. and rickety trailer. I had to load up all of the books myself, as my wife had to watch the kids at home (and she was pissed – ha!). I sweated all of the way home, hoping that the weight of the books did not overheat the truck's engine, or break the axle on the old trailer.

Well, five hours later, I rolled into the driveway, and I unloaded all of the book boxes into our basement. Sheesh. The boxes filled half of the basement. Anyway, I went through all of the books, and there were a lot of penny books in the lot… but, there was also an $80 book that sold several months later, and five or six $50 books. There were also another 80 books that I listed on Amazon for $3-20. All in all, I probably listed $600-700 worth of books into my Amazon inventory.

It actually was more time and work than I liked to get rid of the rest of the books, but I made another couple of hundred dollars by grouping categories of books together and then listing them as book lots on eBay. I also sold several other single books on eBay for another $50, or so. It was a pretty good investment for a $50 auction and $50 in gas. I almost made the eBay auction investment back with one $80 book sale!

Several months later, I bought a 10,000 item music lot on eBay for $700. This was the steal of the decade! I ended up listing over 12,000 items on Amazon (there were considerably more items than were advertised) at an average price of over $8.50. There were a lot of rare CDs and vinyl records in that lot. I also sold another hundred items on eBay.

By the time I had listed all of the items in that lot six months later, I had jump-started my Amazon business. My inventory jumped from a modest 1,500 items to over 11,000 items, and the average price stayed at about $8 an item.

Yes, I had to rent a U-Haul trailer and haul the lot from five hours away. I also lost the use of my garage and part of my basement for several months, and my wife and I spent a lot of free time listing items on Amazon.

But, by the time all of the items were listed on Amazon, I went from selling 4-5 items on Amazon for $50 a week to selling 10-20 items a week for a consistent $100-250, and considerably more around Christmas.

There you have it. The true story of how I built a $50,000-$70,000 Amazon inventory in my spare time. By buying used items at garage sales, thrift stores, and online and large bulk lots of goods, I kept my expenditures at a very minimal level for the projected return.

I was able to build my Amazon business in my spare time at my own pace. A lot of the "work" was done after working at my full-time job during the day, and then settling down on the couch or on the deck and while enjoying a cool beverage.

Now, I have built an Amazon business that will continue to pay for my efforts for a long time, with very little maintenance. You have to love passive income! Down the line, I may also opt to sell my Amazon business for $20 or 30K, and make a down payment on a vacation home. We will see what happens!

Chapter Summary:

What I learned in my first year of Amazon selling:

- The most important thing is not initial sales. Start building your inventory and worry about the number of sales later.

- Start by getting used items for free or buying at very low prices

- Sell free items that you already have in your home

- Look for 'high-profit' items

- Buy cheap items at garage sales and thrift stores.

- Look for large lots of low priced items to break up into single Amazon inventory items

- Flipping eBay listings to Amazon – Lots and Single items

BREAKING IT DOWN: CATEGORIES OF USED ITEMS TO SELL

I would like to talk to you about what to look for while you are shopping for inventory items at garage sales, yard sales, flea markets and thrift stores and provide you with some tips that will help you to find high value items at very low prices.

In this chapter, there will be hyperlinks provided to my website Garage Sale Academy. These links are provided to provide you with in-depth information, and to save me from having to reinvent the wheel.

The information is already spelled out in detail on a variety of webpages, so why should I waste your time by making you read it twice, right? Having said that, this book relies on readers using the hyperlinks to navigate to related GSA pages, as that is where all of the step-by-step instructions for buying and selling specific types of used items are located.

There are also photographs and helpful links to other free sites on each topic.

Books: (Details on Garage Sale Academy Selling Used Books and Amazon Textbooks)

Books are easy to sell on Amazon and can be very profitable, which is why so many existing Amazon sellers specialize in selling them. Books are available at almost every yard sale and thrift store, and they are usually affordable. Plus, some older books are collectible and valuable. You will regularly find $20 books wherever you look for Amazon inventory.

The GSA Used Books page has many tips for how to find high priced books to add to your inventory, but here are some highlights:

- Use a Smart Phone with the Amazon Price Check application. This takes the guess-work out of deciding which used books to buy for profit. You scan the book with your Smart phone, and the app tells you what the book is selling for on Amazon. Links are available for the app on GSA.

- Used textbooks can be sold for excellent profits. If you have bought textbooks lately, you know that even used texts can cost $150. But, you have to be careful buying textbooks without the Amazon Price Check app. Many titles are updated yearly, so if you have a textbook that is two or three years old, it may be outdated and worthless.

- Many sellers look for hardcover books and textbooks to sell for profit, but I have well over 100 softcover books in my Amazon inventory worth over $50, and several over $100. Look for rare titles, softcover texts, vintage pulp fiction titles, and very thin books. Many of these vintage books with less than 40 pages are rare and collectible.

- If you look at a book and think "Who in the heck would want to read that?!", it is probably rare and valuable. Buy it. Some of the highest priced books in my inventory are not first edition classics, they are rare paperbacks: Flood Hazards in Virginia - $195, The Thrift Store Prospector - $195.60, Answers to the Space Flight Challenge - $145. All three of these books are thin vintage softcover books found for under $1.

- Condition is very important. Books with condition problems like broken hinges, missing pages, and modern books with missing dust jackets can make the books worthless for resale.

- Check all free boxes for books and media items. Take EVERY book that you can find for free. The worst case scenario is that you have to donate the book to Goodwill later. I have found many $20 books in free boxes.

Music: (Details on Garage Sale Academy Selling Used CDs and Selling Used Media

Used music such as CDs, vinyl records and even 8-tracks, cassettes, and other vintage formats can be sold on Amazon. Some collectible vinyl record and CD titles can be worth thousands of dollars, but it is very rare to find these at second-hand stores.

Selling used music is a competitive business. Everybody loves music. Still, you can make good money selling used CDs and records, if you know what to look for and how to sell them. Many used music internet sellers hang out on eBay for some reason, which gives Amazon sellers a big advantage.

Amazon allows you to list inventory for free. EBay also has tens of thousands of used music items at auction at any given time. Tons of quality items never get bids on eBay. The same item can be listed for free on Amazon, sell for a higher price, and sellers are given a $3.99 shipping credit.

Here is a selection of helpful tips for buying used music for profit:

- Don't be tempted to buy music that you like for $2+. Many popular titles on CD are 'penny CDs'. Remember, millions of these CDs were printed, and many CDs are being tossed in favor of MP3 files. There is an overabundance of many pop titles at second hand locations and on Amazon, which makes many excellent used CDs almost worthless to sell on Amazon.

- Use Amazon Price Check app.

- Look for rare CDs, and classical titles. Vintage blues and jazz CDs can also be valuable.

- Pick up any CDs that are sealed and you can sell on Amazon as 'New'.

- Grab any CDs that you see in free boxes. Even CDs without cases can be sold on Amazon.

- Check all CDs before you buy them. Ensure that the CD is in the case, as thieves often steal the disc and leave the case, especially at thrift stores. Also, check for large surface scratches, missing artwork, and broken case hinges.

- Keep a supply of replacement cases on hand. I often swap out cases with broken hinges, broken CD holders, or surface cracks.

Video Games and DVDs (Details on [GSA Selling Used Video Games](#) and [Selling Used DVDs](#))

Used video games can be excellent sellers on Amazon! It is common to find used video game systems for $10 or less at second-hand locations, and many vintage systems will sell for $30-70 when packaged with the cords, controllers and a couple of games.

It would be well worth your time to scan through the video game system category on Amazon, so that you have a good idea what each system is currently selling for.

Become familiar with what the power cords and AV cords for video game systems look like, so you can pick them up when you see them at garage sales or thrift stores. I have found a lot of cords for 25 cents at garage sales, packed in with big bags of cords at thrift stores, and even in free boxes. You never know when you will find a system that is missing a cord.

Just last week, I found an original PlayStation at a thrift store for $4. It had no cords or controllers with it, which is why it was priced so cheaply. I took it home, dug through my 'random cords box', and found a PlayStation 1 power cord, AV cord and two controllers.

I found all of these accessories in free boxes at garage sales over the years. I tested the PlayStation, and it worked great. I listed it on Amazon and it sold yesterday for $25. If I would have had some PS1 games to package with the system, I could have earned another $5 to $10.

Both DVDs and video games are constantly upgrading in technology. The newest video game system titles can bring $40 used and sell the same day that Amazon sellers list them. That is why it can really pay to have your Smart phone with you. These newer video games will not be $1 or $2. But, even if you have to pay $10 for a $30 title with high demand, you win.

DVDs are getting harder to make money on. Many tech-savvy consumers are opting to buy movies by streaming them on their computers, and most people now get movies sent to their homes via Netflix.

This is especially true of newer titles that are available in Blu-ray. Many used standard DVDs are penny DVDs, when the same title is now available on Blu-ray.

Look for older DVDs that were not re-released on Blu-ray. Popular TV series DVD sets also sell well. We hit a home run about three years ago when the local hospital gave their nurses free copies of vintage TV show DVD sets. Several of our friends gave us their copies, and we found quite a few more at thrift stores, still in the shrink-wrap. Several of the sets sold for almost $100, and the single episodes sold for $20-30. Bingo!

Some other DVDs to look for: Director's cuts, Collector's Sets of popular titles and classics, Remastered DVDs, rare titles that you have never heard of, cult classics, and vintage sports DVDs. I have also done very well with rare concert DVDs, especially if you can find early concerts of popular bands or punk rock / thrash concerts.

You can also occasionally make some money on rare VHS tapes, but they sell slowly and most of them are not worth much. If you can get them for free… take them, of course.

Used Toys and Board Games:

Selling used toys and games on Amazon is a nice racket. Very few people know that you can sell these used items on Amazon. The great thing is that often, you cannot sell these items on eBay and make a profit, either. So, the few of us Amazon sellers who know about selling used toys on Amazon are the only ones buying these items to sell.

You can sell almost every modern used toy in decent condition on Amazon, as long as you have either A) a bar code or B) the actual name of the toy (which is often more difficult to figure out than you might think).

Pay attention to the toys aisles while you are at Meijer, K-Mart and Wal-Mart so that you know what toys are titled, and which toys are expensive to buy at stores. Those are the toys that you will look for while at second-hand stores and garage sales.

Even loose action figures, Hot Wheels, Barbie dolls, and other small toys can be sold in used condition. Used toys can often take some time to sell, but you can also get these toys for very cheap. If you have young kids like we do, outgrown toys can become profit makers in your Amazon inventory, especially large outdoor toys and electronic toys.

We have sold many used toys that our boys have outgrown. Kids also learn about the value of keeping toys in good condition. We let our boys sell their own toys to upgrade to new ones, but the toys that are in poor condition or missing pieces… sorry, boys.

Used board games can also be sold fairly effectively on Amazon. Some are worth $50+. In the last couple of years, I have sold four sealed board games found at thrift stores for over $50, including an original Trivial

Pursuit for $80 that was sold in two days. The vintage 3M bookshelf games also sell for good profits – usually over $20.

Some other games to look for: electronic board games, vintage versions of classic games, and handheld electronic games.

Household and Decorative Items:

As we discussed before, almost anything with a barcode can be sold on Amazon. If you see items at garage sales that are still in the original packaging and it has a barcode, it can be listed in seconds and will probably yield profits.

I have sold a wide array of used household items found at garage sales and thrift stores. Newer decorative items that are sold at popular department stores often sell fairly quickly on Amazon. My wife has even sold new handbags that she bought on clearance at Kohl's, and doubled her purchase price on almost every Amazon sale.

Some categories of items that I have sold on Amazon and made good money: electronics, prints, utensils, clocks, and holiday decorations (Halloween décor sells for higher prices than Christmas, for some reason).

Understand that many used household items sell very slowly, and you will have to store them for a while. Many of these items are larger and bulkier than media items, so you will need more room than you would for books or CDs.

Chapter Summary:

Types of used items that can be found for cheap and sold on Amazon for high profit margins:

- Books
- Music
- Video Games
- Toys and Games
- Household Items
- New sealed items with barcodes

INCREASE PROFITS AND SELL ITEMS FASTER BY MAKING BETTER ITEM DESCRIPTIONS ON AMAZON

It never ceases to amaze me how lazy some people are. I always look at other sellers' item descriptions while I am listing my own items. There are many sellers who do not even bother to type in a description of their item, or its condition!

A typical Amazon item page will have dozens of listings from sellers. There are only two things that customers can look at to determine which Amazon seller that they will buy the item from.

The first is the seller's rating, which is displayed beside the seller's name. We will talk about seller ratings and your reputation on Amazon later.

The second thing that Amazon customers look at is the item description.

Keep in mind that there are typically multiple listings that will be priced within $1 of each other, so the item description is often what sells the item to the costumer. Still, there many listings that do not have a description at all, just a condition listing and price.

For us small to medium sized Amazon sellers, that is a huge advantage. Many companies with huge inventories do not take the time to make effective item description. By only taking less than 30 seconds, you can set your listing apart from the other listings and make it much more likely to sell. Here is how.

Let's take this step by step, using an example. We will list a copy of "The Hobbit" that I have in my personal collection for sale on Amazon.

1. First, we find the correct Amazon item page. There are many versions of The Hobbit, so we will enter a text description – 'The Hobbit 1967 hardcover'. We scan through the search results and find the exact title, with the same dust jacket art. Select that listing

2. Look through the existing listings from other sellers and determine the price that you want to sell your copy for. I usually price my items at the low end of the listings for each item condition. In other words, for "The Hobbit", there will be many listings for each condition subcategory. The lowest existing price for my book in the 'Used – Very Good' subcategory is $8.85. I may list my book at $8.80.

3. Start your item description by verifying that the copy that you have is the exact item for that description page. This gives customers confidence that they are getting exactly what they want. My description would start with this: 'The Hobbit by Tolkien, 1967 hardcover book with dust jacket. 2nd Edition, 4th Print, illustrated. Dust jacket art as seen above'.

4. Describe the condition of the book. Do <u>not</u> rely simply on the Amazon condition guidelines. Most customers do have any idea what the guidelines are. Remember, your reputation is at stake, so make sure that your customers know what they are buying. The second part of the description would be: 'Interior VG. No marks, missing pgs, etc. Jacket G –several chips at edges, one repaired split to back. No other stickers, marks. Binding like new.'

5. Give the customer even more confidence by giving them a short sales pitch. This should be saved as a text document, so that you can cut-and-paste it into each Amazon listing: 'Reliable and experienced book seller with thousands of satisfied customers. Items are securely packaged using dedicated book mailers in bubble wrap. International and Expedited orders welcome.'

This whole listing would take you no more than 20-30 seconds to type and/or cut-and-paste. Yet, this listing will make your item much more likely to sell to the first couple of customers looking to buy "The Hobbit" in used condition.

One thing to note is that you only have a certain amount of characters that will be displayed to buyers on the initial item page. If you have a long description, only the first part of the description will be seen, and the customer would have to click on the 'More' link to see the rest of the description.

Try to get the most important information displayed on the initial screen. Make sure that verification of the item and the most important condition description(s) are visible from the item listing page, without the customer having to click anything.

If the customer is interested in your item listing, they will usually click on the 'More' link to read the rest of your description.

Chapter Summary:

It is important to write good item descriptions

- Earn more sales by building customer confidence
- Prevent non-positive customer feedback

What does a good Amazon item description contain?
1. Verify item – Identification numbers, titles
2. Thorough condition description(s)

3. Build confidence in your business – safe shipping, experience
4. Keep important information first

PRICING AND INVENTORY MANAGEMENT PRACTICES THAT YIELD MORE AMAZON SALES

Let's face it. Most people who buy used items do so in order to save some money over buying new items. What does that mean for the used item seller on Amazon?

In my opinion, you must price items to move. That means that many items should be priced at the lower end of the price range for the applicable condition subcategory for each item that is listed. About 75% of my inventory items are the lowest priced item in their condition subcategory.

On the surface, this may seem to be counterproductive to profits. Really, this strategy works well for several reasons. Number one, impulse buyers are going to pick the lowest priced used item for many items, even if there are a couple more minor condition issues. Number two, customers who choose the lowest priced items are not as picky as the customers who choose to upgrade to higher priced offerings. You will have fewer customer returns and negative feedbacks from customers who buy the lowest priced item that is offered.

This does not mean that if you have a high-priced collectible that is in excellent condition that you should lose profits by listing your item below inferior products. This 'lowest price principle' only applies to identical items that are comparable in condition.

One trick that I have used for rare items with only a couple of listings is to set the price far above the lowest price. For instance, if I had a rare CD that only had one listing at $4.99, I often will list my copy at $24.95. I have sold many items this way, as long as the description identifies the item well and specifies that it is collectible and rare. Sometimes, the $24.95 item will even sell before the $4.95 item, because the customer thinks that there is something wrong with the lower priced item. Even if the lower priced item sells first, you will still have the next lowest priced item at $24.95, so the next customer will have no choice – your $24.95 item, or nothing. Works great.

Professional Seller Account owners have the ability to make additions to the Amazon marketplace for items that are not available. I have probably made over 100 of these additions for rare books, vinyl records, CDs and other collectibles. The process is easy. You enter details for the item, upload a digital photograph, and then describe your item condition to list it into your inventory.

If I have to make an addition, I assume that the item is rare (or it would have already been on the Amazon marketplace, right?). If I have to make an addition for an item, I never price the inventory item below $20. Often, I will price the item at $50 or $100. Usually, even when other Amazon sellers list their items on item pages that I have added, they will price their items based on my price – perhaps $1 under mine.

More often than not, if you have to make an addition, nobody will find a copy of that item for a long time. I have sold many items that I have made listing pages for between $50 and $100. Sometimes, they sell quickly, as if people were looking for the item, but had previously been unable to find one.

You will have to manage your inventory periodically to keep your prices competitive with other sellers' listings. After you have been adding items for a while, you will find that items that you listed as the lowest prices item in its condition subcategory are $1 or $2 above the lowest price. It is very common for other sellers to do exactly what you do… set the lowest price by condition.

There are three ways that you can look at this situation. Number one, you can take an aggressive pricing tact, and use Amazon's 'price match' option. There is a check-box on each listing page that allows you to match the lowest price by item, or by condition subcategory. You can use this option for some higher priced items, but be careful using it for low priced items. All it takes is for one idiot to price their item at a penny. Then you are stuck only making a couple of cents on the shipping credit, if somebody buys your item for a penny because of the price match.

The second pricing approach is to set your own price and not adjust it, regardless of what other sellers do. This approach also has risks. You will lose some $50 to other Amazon sellers, when they undercut your low price by a penny. Despite the risks of losing some sales, this is the easiest approach to use for experienced sellers with large inventories. Besides, you have an advantage over many of your competitors if you write item descriptions as we have discussed and observe the customer relations advice in the next chapter (you will have higher ratings than most used items sellers).

The third approach is a hybrid between the two approaches we have already talked about. With this approach, you adjust your item prices periodically. Most of the time, you will be reducing your price by only a couple of pennies, but you will be the lowest priced item again. You will get the most sales on Amazon if you are the lowest priced used item.

Using this approach, you MUST force yourself to adjust your prices according to a schedule, as adjusting your prices is the most boring and time consuming task Amazon sellers have to do. Finding inventory is enjoyable. Listing items at good prices is rewarding. Adjusting your inventory prices sucks, but it is beneficial.

By the time you get to several thousand items in your inventory, it will take you a long time to get through all of your items. Adjusting prices is easy. You go to your 'manage inventory' under the 'inventory' tab. Then, you only have to change the prices from the list. You do not have to access individual item pages to adjust prices. However, when you have to change hundreds or thousands of items, it can take a very long time.

You can also update several pages of inventory prices at a time, rather than adjusting your entire inventory at once. Using this method, you will not keep your inventory prices as up-to-date, but it allows you break up the monotony of adjusting your entire inventory at once.

When I began selling on Amazon, I was updating my prices about every other week. It's easy to accomplish the task, when you do not have many inventory items.

Now, I would say that I use a combination of approach #2 and #3. Now that I have an inventory of almost 8200 items, I have a pretty good flow of inventory items off of my shelves. I know that if I updated my prices more often, I would increase sales. But, updating my inventory would take days, if I were to do it all at once.

Time spent updating my inventory is time that I do not have to find additional inventory items or spend on other projects, like writing books.

With over 8200 items, I have 33 pages of items with 250 items displayed per page. I tend to update about five pages every other week. Also, I update my entire inventory at least twice a year.

Now that I have been selling on Amazon for a while, I think that my items often sell before other sellers' listings when the prices are comparable, anyway. If customers look at seller stats, they can see that I am an experienced Amazon seller, and my positive feedback percentage is very high for a used item seller. I do not feel that I have to lower prices as much now as I used to when I began selling on Amazon.

Chapter Summary:

How to price your used items: Lowest price in condition subcategory sells more items and turns inventory over to make room for new items.

Approaches for inventory pricing management

1. Maintain the lowest price in the condition subcategory – Price matching
2. Set your best prices when you list items, and leave them
3. Hybrid – Limited price matching

CUSTOMER RELATIONS PRACTICES AND MAINTAINING A HIGH CUSTOMER FEEDBACK PERCENTAGE

There is no difference between the manner in which you would treat a customer at a physical store and the way you should treat Amazon buyers. Keeping your customers happy is vital to your Amazon business. As we discussed in prior chapters, your Amazon positive feedback percentage is one of the first things that your potential customers will look at when deciding whether to buy goods from you.

Let's take a step back and I will explain Amazon's feedback process and what feedback means for your business.

Most people are familiar with the idea of feedback for internet purchases. EBay has been using customer feedback for years and it is integrated into their buying process. Amazon's feedback process is not as prominent in their business model, as Amazon was originally designed primarily for selling new factory-sealed goods, while eBay has always been seen as an outlet for selling used and collectible items.

With the Amazon feedback model, customers are able to leave feedback for every transaction that they complete through Amazon, but feedback is not requested by Amazon. Buyers have to access their customer order page to find the link to leave feedback. Many Amazon buyers do not even know that there is a feedback system for Amazon purchases. I receive customer feedback on less than 10% of my transactions.

Customers often don't think about leaving feedback... unless there is a problem with their order, or they receive an item that exceeds their expectations.

"Listen to me now, and believe me later", as Hans and Franz said in Saturday Night Live... Protect your feedback percentage at all costs. Do NOT take negative and neutral feedbacks lightly. If you do receive negative feedback, make every effort to contact your buyer and come to an agreement whereby they will remove their negative feedback.

Amazon provides a link with every transaction, so that you can contact your buyer. There is also a link provided from your Seller Feedback page. I recommend the following approach when contacting customers... kiss butt.

Whoever said that "the customer is always right" is full of crap. 95% of the time, they are wrong. Most of the time, it is the customer who made the mistake by ordering items from the wrong category or buying items without reading the condition description.

Still, in order to protect your feedback rating, you have to appease jaded customers. Be overly friendly. Apologize. Explain your position without sounding condescending. I have had very good luck using the following process after receiving neutral or negative feedback.

First, contact the customer as soon as possible. With your first message, apologize for any misunderstanding, and ask them what you can do to resolve the situation. If there is a disagreement in the condition described or the item's assigned condition, provide the customer with the condition guidelines and explain why you assigned that condition to the item in question. Explain that assigning conditions is subjective for used items and people often disagree, but that you did your best to describe the condition. Provide them with the process for removing feedback, so that they can voluntarily remove the feedback. I cut-and-paste the instructions from the Amazon help page.

If there is still a problem after the initial message is sent, or if the customer does not respond, I send a second message several days later. In the second message, I apologize again, and offer to refund the entire order and not require the customer to send the item back provided they remove their negative feedback. Make sure that you give them the feedback removal instructions again.

Most customers will remove their feedback, especially when you make it financially attractive with the second message. Remember, your feedback rating is very important, and even if you have to take a $20 loss, you will be much further ahead in the long run if you can get a negative feedback removed.

When you sell used items on Amazon, you WILL receive non-positive feedbacks. It is just a question of when it is going to happen. As I mentioned before, even the best sellers of used items get negative feedbacks. This is due in part to the nature of selling used items and the requirement of assigning subjective values, and partly because there are just a number of stupid people out there. Some people just are not going to be happy, no matter what you do. So be prepared to deal with the non-positive feedback(s), because you will receive them eventually.

Here are some steps that you can take to minimize negative feedbacks:

1. Accurately assign condition ratings. When in doubt, assign Used – Good instead of Used – Very Good. Describe condition issues completely in the text description when listing your items.

2. Answer your seller messages, ASAP. Amazon sends you a copy of messages from buyers to your registered email account, and you can also view your messages from your Amazon Seller Home page. When you get messages, respond immediately. Nothing pisses off people more than getting ignored.

3. Deal with non-positive feedbacks immediately, using the procedure described.

4. Don't list items with major flaws. I don't buy anything that I think should be rated as 'Used – Acceptable', which is the lowest condition rating. Don't list anything that you would not like to receive in the mail yourself.

5. Put yourself in your potential customers' shoes. What would you want to know about the item before buying it? What aspects of the condition of the item would you want described to you? Make sure that you address these concerns in your item description.

6. Do not list your item in the wrong category! I see this all of the time when listing used vinyl records. Sellers list CDs in the Vinyl Record category because there is not an existing item page for some rare CDs. Not only is this misleading for customers, it is a violation of Amazon policy and you can get banned from selling on Amazon.

7. Package your items securely, so they do not get damaged during shipping.

8. Consider enclosing a message with each item shipped, or send buyers a personal email with your logo on it. Explain how important customer satisfaction is to your business, and ask them to contact you if there are any condition issues prior to leaving feedback. I have always been undecided on whether to send additional messages regarding feedback. On one hand, you are showing your concern for customer satisfaction. On the other hand, you may be creating more problems for yourself by suggesting that there may possibly be issues with your product(s).

Chapter Summary:

It is vital to your Amazon business to keep customers happy!

1. Builds your business' reputation – High feedback rating = more sales
2. Earn return customers and word-of-mouth advertising
3. Reduces item returns and refunds

How to deal with unhappy customers

1. Return e-mails and messages ASAP
2. Kiss butt and show concern for their issue(s)

How to handle non-positive feedback (This is super important!)

1. Immediate e-mail message
2. Kiss butt, apologize, and tell the customer you value their opinion
3. Explain the value of your feedback rating, and how non-positive feedbacks significantly affect your business. Provide the 'Remove Feedback' instructions
4. If #3 does not work, send a second e-mail that offers a full refund and do not require return of the item, in exchange for feedback removal.

DIVERSIFYING YOUR AMAZON BUSINESS: SELLING PRODUCTS ON CRAIGSLIST, EBAY AND ETSY

A good internet seller does not limit themselves to selling on only one venue. There are many different ways to sell used items, and sellers can take advantage of the benefits each location provides.

Although I believe that Amazon is by far the best overall location to sell the types of goods that I sell, there are times when it is easier or more productive to sell my items on sites other than Amazon.

For instance, there are going to be times when you want to sell items with a quick turnaround. Perhaps you have a family vacation coming up, or you want to make a large purchase.

EBay almost guarantees a sale within a week, if you set the starting price low enough to encourage bidding. You can even make your auction shorter to decrease the time it takes to get payment for your items – you can make 3-Day or even 1-Day listings.

EBay also has the following benefits, when compared to selling on Amazon:

1. Often shorter time to get your money – 1 day to 1 week.

2. There is always the potential to have your auction make more money than you thought the item was worth. If you get the right situation and have multiple bidders who really want your item, you can make a lot of extra money.

3. Visually appealing items benefit from additional photos on eBay

4. Some categories of items cannot be sold on Amazon, or sell very slowly. For instance, vintage used clothing can make a lot of money on eBay, but cannot be sold on Amazon.

5. You can set your own shipping fees on eBay. Some items have insufficient shipping allowances on Amazon. You sometimes end up eating profit to make up for the shipping shortage on Amazon.

I use eBay infrequently, but there are definitely advantages to listing items in an auction setting there from time to time.

Etsy.com is another internet location that specializes is vintage items, arts and crafts and craft supplies. Etsy is an excellent location to sell retro and mid-century items, which you can often find at garage sales for cheap. These items can sell for hundreds of dollars on Etsy. Etsy is set up much like eBay Fixed Price listings. You make a listing like on eBay, and provide photos. Your listing is active for 3 months for twenty cents.

For further discussion on the benefits of Amazon, Etsy and eBay, see the Garage Sale Academy page eBay Selling Alternative.

I also use Craigslist for selling large items that would cost too much to ship on Amazon or eBay. Craigslist listings are free, and there is also the advantage to avoiding the hassle of packaging and shipping large or very fragile items.

Chapter Summary:

How and when to diversify your used item sales using other websites

1. eBay – see below

2. Etsy for vintage, retro, and arts & crafts

3. Craigslist for large, heavy, or very fragile items to avoid shipping

When eBay may be a better choice to sell used items:

1. Certain used items cannot be sold effectively on Amazon e.g. Used clothes
2. Visually appealing collectibles benefit from more photos and more detailed descriptions
3. When you think that an eBay auction setting may yield many bids and possibly a higher price than a set price Amazon listing
4. When Amazon's shipping allowance does not cover actual shipping costs – set your own shipping fees on your eBay auction.
5. When you want money fast. eBay auctions end in 1,3,5, or 7 days (10 days at a higher list price).

ADDITIONAL LINKS FOR FURTHER RESEARCH

Eric Michael Author Central Page

Garage Sale Academy Webpages:

1. Garage Sale Academy Blog
2. Garage Sale Academy Home Page
3. Garage Sale Talk Forum
4. Almost Free Money Books
5. Flipping Garage Sale Finds
6. How to Sell on Amazon – Amazon Selling Tips
7. Amazon Shipping and Packaging
8. Selling on Etsy
9. How to Sell on eBay
10. Selling Used Books
11. Selling Amazon Textbooks
12. Selling Used Media Items
13. Selling Used DVDs

14. Selling Used Video Games

15. Selling Used CDs

16. Thrift Shop Flipping

17. Free Gold at Garage Sales (How to Find Free Items to Sell)

18. Top 10 Garage Sale Items to Sell

Related Book Titles in the Almost Free Money series:

Almost Free Money, volume 1: How to Make Significant Money on Free Items That You Can Find Anywhere, Including Garage Sales, Scrap Metal, and Discarded Items

#1 Amazon Kindle Bestseller: Learn how to find many free items and other items that cost under $1 and sell them online from home for excellent profits. Includes: Flipping garage sale and yard treasure, selling scrap metal, finding precious metals like gold and silver in vintage discarded items for free, selling used items on eBay and Amazon, building passive income streams, how to process your home to find many items to sell online, a virtual trip to a scrap metal dealer, and how to search garage sales, thrift stores, and flea markets for the best items to sell.

Almost Free Money has appendices that contain over 540 items that can be sold and specifies where to sell them for maximum profit with numeric and textual eBay categories.

Almost Free Money Reviews

"I thoroughly enjoyed the ideas and strategies in this book. If you are a go getter and have some time to hit yard sales, thrift shops, and a few other places the author suggests this book could make you some extra money. I have always been interested in the scrap metal business. The author describes how he breaks down household items to find metals like copper and gold. Very creative stuff.

"This is a great book! It contains lots of ideas on how to make money from surprising places, and the resource directory at the back of the book is worth 10x the price of this book all by itself. Highly recommended."

"This is a great book! Detailed and practical. Not theory - FACT! Eric really gives you everything you need. Recession? What Recession? If you learn how to do this, you'll always have a fall back plan. There will always be a need for scrap metal and this book shows you how to get it for nothing or almost nothing. Five Stars! My highest recommendation!"

Garage Sale Superstar Description:

Would you like to Double or Triple your Garage Sale or Yard Sale profits, without spending any money?

Have you heard stories about people making over $1000 at garage sales, and wished for similar success? Have you ever wondered how to effectively price your items that you will be selling at your garage sale?

How would you like to be able to design a free garage sale advertisement that will pull garage sale shoppers in to your sale from other cities and counties?

Would you like to know what types of belongings sell for the most money at garage sales, so that you can round them up from your own home?

Would you like to make the process of organizing your garage sale easier and more fun? Have you ever thought about selling some of your collectible items on the internet to make more money, but did not know how to get started?

Garage Sale Superstar provides solutions to all of these questions asked by almost every single garage sale or yard sale host. In Superstar, the second book in the Almost Free Money series, detailed instructions are provided for making excellent money by selling your used property at free venues like garage sales, yard sales, estate sales, and tag sales. As a veteran of visiting over 1,000 garage sales in the last ten years, I can provide specific examples of what works for garage sale hosts, and what does not.

Here are the Top Ten Benefits from reading Garage Sale Superstar:

Learn garage sale techniques used by the most successful garage sale hosts to rake in thousands of dollars at their personal garage sales.

Learn how to maximize your garage sale for either higher profits or more items sold. Determine whether you want max sales, or clearing clutter to clean out your home or garage.

Ensure that you have a SAFE garage sale. You would be surprised how many hosts neglect their family's safety, or the safety of kids visiting their sales.

Learn how to arrange your displays and tables, one of the most important aspects of maximizing garage sale and yard sale profits.

Make your own free garage sale advertisements that will make people flock to your sale, with zero advertising fees.

Learn what to put in your ads, where to post them, and how to spice up your classified ads with photos or graphics.

Learn what days of the week to be open, and what hours are peak selling times. What time should your garage sale be open in the morning?

We have some innovative ideas for making garage sales inviting to potential shoppers, and passers-by on your street. They are also fun for hosts and their children.

Discover what types of items are collectible and should be sold on eBay to make significantly more money.

Do you hate the process of organizing your garage sale? Learn how to make it fun by including your friends and family. Organize your garage sale items, while socializing or perhaps over several adult drinks.

These free garage sale tips work anywhere in the world. Anybody can do this!

Fast Cash: Selling Used Items for Profit Description:

Learn how to build an excellent supplementary income or start a new home business by selling used items!

Fast Cash discusses how to process second-hand locations to find the best low cost items to sell for great profits. Learn how to find the most treasure at garage sales, yard sales, thrift stores, and flea markets. The Fast Cash system is a great source of income for internet entrepreneurs, stay-at-home parents, retired seniors, and people with disabilities.

Learn how to process the items you sell to make them sell for higher prices.

Learn how to sell your item for higher profits on eBay and Amazon by building the best possible auction page or item description listing. Learn how to provide the most effective photographs to entice bidders and buyers. Learn how to make a title that gets clicks from potential buyers.

THANK YOU, READERS!

Thank you for taking the time to read this book. I hope that you enjoyed it as much as I enjoyed writing it.

Please put your mind to immediately applying what you learned in this book. Don't wait until next week to start! You can find items to sell in any location, and at any time of the year.

YOU have to make up your mind to start selling used items on Amazon, and it will be all increasing profits from there. I wish you success in building your passive income through Amazon.

Click on the link below to join the Almost Free Money Nation. This free newsletter provides exclusive free white papers and advance reading chapters from unreleased AFM books, free tips and tricks to help you find great items at second-locations and learn how to sell them, and links to new Garage Sale Academy webpages.

http://forms.aweber.com/form/75/228725575.htm

If you have any questions, please contact me at the Almost Free Money Facebook page and the Garage Sale Academy Facebook page, on Twitter, or email me at almostfreemoney@yahoo.com. I would enjoy hearing from you!

If you feel that this book has helped you to find new and enjoyable ways to make a new passive income for you and your family, I humbly ask you for only two things. #1, tell your family and friends about this book, and #2, please take several seconds to leave positive feedback for this book on its Amazon Detail Page. After all, you should be able to easily make 1000 times the $3 that you spent on this book in your first year of selling.

Positive feedback directly affects other readers' reviews and leads to additional orders, and the proceeds from this book will go directly into my sons' college funds. Thanks again, and happy hunting!

ALMOST FREE MONEY

How to Make Significant Money from Free Materials You Can Find Anywhere, Including Garage Sales, Scrap Metal, and Discarded Items

Copyright, Legal Notice and Disclaimer:

This publication is protected under the US Copyright Act of 1976 and all other applicable international, federal, state and local laws, and all rights are reserved, including resale rights: you are not allowed to give or sell this Guide to anyone else.

Please note that much of this publication is based on personal experience and anecdotal evidence. Although the author and publisher have made every reasonable attempt to achieve complete accuracy of the content in this document, they assume no responsibility for errors or omissions. Also, you should use this information as you see fit, and at your own risk. Your particular situation may not be exactly suited to the examples illustrated here; in fact, it's likely that they won't be the same, and you should adjust your use of the information and recommendations accordingly.

Any trademarks, service marks, product names or named features are assumed to be the property of their respective owners, and are used only for reference. There is no implied endorsement if we use one of these terms.

Finally, use your head. Nothing in this Guide is intended to replace common sense, legal, medical or other professional advice, and is meant to inform and entertain the reader.

Copyright © 2013 Eric Michael. All rights reserved worldwide

Passive Income for Life

© Almost Free Money, Volume 5

PREFACE

The purpose of this document is to provide the motivated person with a variety of ways to make some quick, easy money with very little initial investment. There are hundreds of sources of income lying around your house, or on your property right now. There are hundreds more available for free in your community, if you are willing to talk to people and do some leg-work.

If you have already heard about this book, the temptation is going to be to skip right to the Appendices, but do yourself a favor and resist the urge. You need to have a basic understanding of how to handle your business and how to effectively process items and materials before you start latching onto your swag.

You should learn how to identify good targets on your own, before limiting yourself to the 520 items that I have found for free and sold. After reading this book, you will be able to immediately spot good sources of free money. When you see broken electronics, lamps, grills, vehicles, and bikes along the roadway, you will know the value of the parts and where to sell them for maximum profits. You will also know exactly what to look for at garage sales, thrift stores and flea markets.

There are many ways to make extra money, and different avenues appeal to different people. I would suggest that you find a combination of sources that you find interesting and pursue them.

This is not a get-rich-quick scheme. However, you will save yourself and your family money, and have an opportunity for a secondary income using the information in this document. If you are willing to work harder than your competition, you can also start your own small business with very little investment.

Some of these materials can be sold without internet experience, BUT if you want to maximize your profits, you must at least be able to research information online. If you are willing to do some surfing, you will maximize your profits and find many new and exciting sources of free items to sell.

This document provides real-life examples of opportunities that I have taken advantage of in twelve years of selling discarded items for profit. This document's primary goal is to provide many different avenues for profit, and provide background knowledge that allows the reader to decide which sources of income are right for them.

We will discuss many different items and materials to sell, the easiest and most profitable places to sell your finds, and some tips for enhancing your profits and creating your own niche.

The reader will take a "virtual" trip to a scrap metal dealer, where I describe in detail how easy it is to sell scrap metal for the first time by yourself, with no training required. You will also learn the painfully easy process for selling almost any material on the internet at eBay, and on the Amazon Marketplace.

Perhaps most importantly, the reader will learn where to go to conduct their own research and find even more sources of income. Being able to effectively research income sources is the most important aspect of a growing small business. The reader is also provided with a number of links to internet sites with invaluable information on a variety of topics that you can use to make money.

Many of these internet sites were created by businesspersons with decades of knowledge on their particular subjects, and many have made at least six figure incomes in their niches. These sites have outstanding explanations on locating and selling free (or almost free) materials for profit, and most of the sites provide detailed images of what to look for.

If you are a visually-oriented learner, you will be using the hyperlinks provided in this document frequently to refer to applicable internet sites with images, in order to visualize the meaning of the text descriptions in this book.

Also provided to complement this document are appendices that contain over five hundred individual items and materials that you can find anywhere for free (or almost free), and details where to sell them for profit. These printer-friendly lists are broken down into categories: Usable Items, EBay Collectibles, Organic Items, and Items with Defined Values.

To use the EBay category numbers provided within the appendix lists, simply type or cut-and-paste the number into the category box when making your auction on the EBay or Auctiva (an auction listing website discussed later in the document) listing page.

I also provide you with over twenty sources to advance your knowledge base with further reading on the internet.

ABOUT THE AUTHOR

Eric Michael is married and is a proud father of two energetic sons. He enjoys family outings and many outdoor activities, including fishing, hunting and camping.

The information provided in Almost Free Money was compiled after twelve years of internet research and personal experiences developed a unique skill set – the ability to find a diverse selection of free items (or priced under $1) that could be sold on the internet for surprisingly good money.

In that time period, Mr. Michael has sold well over 10,000 unique items that were located for under $1 on the internet at an average price of over $8.50 an item. The Almost Free Money system has given his family the second income necessary to allow a parent to stay at home with his two boys, instead of paying for day care.

He has gone on to develop a popular website titled Garage Sale Academy that incorporates portions of Almost Free Money, and expands into other arenas of profiting from flipping garage sale, thrift store and flea market finds, as well as helping garage sale hosts make maximum cash at their sales. He also hosts Facebook fan pages for Almost Free Money and Garage Sale Academy, as well as a Garage Sale Blog and Forum.

He has also written books in the Almost Free Money series titled Garage Sale Superstar, Fast Cash: Flipping Used Items and recently released the softcover book version of Almost Free Money, which is the easiest way to make use of the information in the appendices.

Click on the link below to join the Almost Free Money Nation. This free newsletter provides exclusive and free white papers and advance reading

chapters from unreleased Almost Free Money series books, free tips and tricks to help you find great items at second-locations and learn how to sell them, and links to new Garage Sale Academy webpages.
http://forms.aweber.com/form/75/228725575.htm

START-UP: INITIAL ASSESSMENT

Before we get into the nuts and bolts of this document, it's important for you to understand several things about yourself. First, what do you hope to accomplish by using this information? Are you looking for a second income? Are you time strapped, and only have time to save your family a little money? Are you considering a new business opportunity?

In my opinion, you should always leave yourself the opportunity to expand your efforts into at least a significant second income. What the heck, it costs you very little money to obtain your selling inventory, and there is the potential to make fairly easy profits. Why not take advantage of that?

I started out buying collectible items at garage sales for 5-25 cents, and then re-selling them on eBay for up to $250 an item. That was a cash cow for a while, but as more and more people found out how easy it was to sell on eBay, the competition got fierce, and the amount of collectibles in the marketplace drove the selling prices down considerably. So, I started researching other ways to diversify, and not rely so much on collectible items.

Now, I prefer selling items that people are always going to need, and also have a value that is determined outside of popular demand. I enjoy finding items for free while I am recreating, and then sell them for easy cash. I mean really, if you're going to have a serious hobby, make it one that actually makes you money. Why throw away big money on a golf course, when you can spend time shopping for investment items, or attempting to locate $1000 valuables with a metal detector on a beach?

As I started adding new avenues for income, I found that I could use my "hobby" as a second income for my family, and my wife could stay home with our young children, instead of working and paying for childcare. Obviously, that was a huge incentive to step it up and go for it.

When we started making significant money, I knew that we needed some kind of business plan. There are thousands of people selling odds and ends on EBay and other places online. The ones that actually make significant money are the people who: #1: ARE NOT LAZY, #2: Are not stupid, and #3: Are resourceful and are willing to do some research.

I started thinking of my second income as a business. I claimed my earnings on my income taxes, so that I could write off business expenses, such as vehicle mileage and meals while I was finding inventory or going to the scrap metal dealer. I kept track of receipts. I knew how much actual profit I was making after subtracting gas cost and eBay listing fees. I wrote off a home office and storage room deductions on my income taxes. All of these things are actually very easy to do, and make you more money for your business.

Even if you are thinking that you are only going to sell some items and materials from around your home, I can guarantee you that if you put some effort into it, you will at least expand into having your family, friends and neighbors save you items that they would normally throw away, and then you, too, will be on your way to an easy second income. So, what I am telling you is, you might as well save yourself even more money and start right off thinking of this as a business.

You have to consider more than just your initial cost and end sales price for an item and/or material that you have sold. The biggest mistake beginners make is not considering the actual cost of selling a particular item.

For instance, consider two potential sales items. The first is a book that you find at a garage sale for 25 cents and then sell for $20 on EBay. The second is a box of insulated electrical cords that you have collected at your house and then sell at the scrap metal dealer for $20. Which is the better sale?

The answer is: It depends! All things being equal, the box of cords is the better deal, because the only time that you had into prepping the cords was about five seconds to cut the plugs off and stuff them into a box. In order to sell the book on EBay, you have to: 1) photograph the book 2) upload the photos 3) type up the listing, and 4) package the item for shipping. Time is money, and you have to take that into account.

However, if you live in a rural area, and the nearest scrap metal dealer is 45 minutes away, you have the additional travel time and gas money to account for. You have to remember that some avenues may seem on the surface to be great deals, but by the time you factor in your time in preparation, hard work and gas money, they may not be your best alternative in making money.

You are looking for things that you enjoy doing anyway, have a renewable supply of, and are comfortable in selling. You also want to be able to sell the items quickly and without an overabundance of preparation time.

The last thing that you have to consider before starting is, how much storage room do you have available to you? There are a lot of items that you can make good profits on that take up a lot of room. Do you have room to disassemble vehicles or appliances on your property? Do you have room in your home for large bookshelves for storing book or music inventory? If not, you will have to concentrate on smaller items to sell, or items that you know that you can sell almost immediately. Your significant other is not going to want to have your stuff lying all over his or her counters or on the floors in your home.

HOW AND WHERE TO SELL

Before you start accumulating items and materials to sell, it is important to have a good idea where you are going to sell it. Finding the good stuff to sell is only half of the battle. You need to know where to go to get top dollar when you go to re-sell it.

In my experience, the best and quickest way to sell most things is to sell them on eBay. While the sales prices on many items have come down over the last five years or so, there is always going to be a market for items that people need, and you can't beat the convenience and potential deals on eBay for the bargain hunter.

Even if you are intimidated by selling on the internet or don't have the desire to do so, you should still be familiar with how eBay works and how to sell an item there. It will not take you long at all in this line of business to figure out that eBay is the best location to sell many different types of materials, including some that you may have previously thought were only sold elsewhere. Scrap metal is an example.

Consider this. If you sell copper to your local scrap metal dealer, you are selling to a middle-man. Your dealer still has to sell your copper again to a metal wholesaler for his business to make any money, so you are therefore offered considerably less for your scrap on the deal, right?

On eBay, you offer the same box of scrap copper to thousands of scrap dealers and investors. The bidding on your lot is determined by the free market and the spot copper price, not by an individual scrap metal dealer, who often has very little competition in his local marketplace. For more information on selling scrap metal on eBay, visit the applicable web page at Garage Sale Academy.com.

Just about anything you can think of that is bought and sold in any physical marketplace is also sold on EBay. We will get further in depth into the world of EBay in later chapters, but just realize for now that EBay gives you the best opportunity to diversify your sales, and the potential for buyers to bid higher on items than you may have thought the item was worth to begin with.

I remember in our first year of internet selling, my wife and I were at a garage sale. We had a few odds and ends that we were going to buy, and my wife saw a cheap looking plastic beer sign in the ten-cent box near the pay table. She picked it out on a whim, and we paid for our stuff and left. The sign was only about 4 x 8" in size, and made of a thin Plexiglas material.

We offered the sign at auction on eBay, starting at 99 cents, and a week later, two competing bidders had raised the ending price to almost $250! The winner e-mailed us and asked if we had any more signs from the beer company that was advertising with the sign my wife had found. He informed us that the beer company was a popular brand in the state that he was from, and that the brewery had gone out of business over twenty years ago. The signs were impossible to find and were very collectible. Who knew?!

SELLING ON EBAY AND AMAZON

I am not going to devote a lot of time in this document to the subject of beginning to sell items online, only because the websites have done such an excellent job of making it easy for anybody to understand the process of listing items.

Both eBay and Amazon have intentionally designed their listing pages so that you can list items regardless of your internet skills and writing abilities. You will typically only have to type a paragraph or two at the most to describe your items, and simple descriptions often are better than profuse flourishing praise for your items, so do not feel bad if you are not a wordsmith.

Both websites also provide tutorials and FAQ's (Frequently Asked Questions) that are linked to the beginning listing pages. These documents are designed so that even if it you have never turned on a computer, you can still figure out how to get an item listed on their sites. Then, once you have listed your first item, it is very easy to list in subsequent sessions. Once you are signed in, eBay provides you with a link from the initial listing page that allows you to bring up several of the last auctions that you designed to use as a template for listing other auctions.

First, we will discuss how to begin selling on eBay. The only equipment that you will need is: A computer with internet access (high speed internet is a huge advantage, but not required), a digital camera, and a scale for weighing items.

We are going to go step-by-step, and list a collectible book that we will pretend that you found in a free box at a garage sale.

First, look at your book. Can you improve its desirability in an auction setting? People bid on items in EBay listings based on two things; the image(s) of the item and your item description. So, if you can make the digital pictures that you take look better by cleaning up your item a bit before taking the photos, by all means, do so. If the book has a vinyl dust jacket, carefully wipe the outer surface to remove any dust and dirt build-up. If there are price stickers that can be peeled off without damaging the surface of the cover, remove them.

Take several pictures of your book, including several photos of the cover, any nice interior illustrations, interesting text, and any condition issues that the bidder will want to see.

Upload the digital photos to your computer. If you have never uploaded photos, EBay provides directions on the process.

When you upload, start a folder for the items you are going to be selling in your 'My Pictures' Folder on your computer, or put it on your desktop, so that you can find the folder easily when you go to download photos to auctions or listing pages.

Go to your computer and log on to the internet, and go to the eBay site. At the top of the page, there is a link for 'Sell'. Click on the link. If you have never sold on eBay, you will need to register, and provide personal and financial information so that you can get paid for your sales through PayPal. PayPal is EBay's payment collection site.

After you have registered or signed in, go the listing page. You may elect to complete the tutorial the first time you sell. It walks you through each segment of the listing page. It is very user-friendly and allows you to quickly move through the listing page.

Make sure that you weigh your item accurately, so that you can provide the weight of the item for shipping purposes. Don't try to estimate the weight, or you will end up either paying for part of the shipping out of your own pocket, or charging too much for shipping and making your customers angry. You may also elect to allow 'Free U.S. shipping' for your item, which alleviates all of these issues altogether. Just make sure that you pick a starting price that is high enough that you make a minimum profit on the item after you add in the shipping costs that you are going to have to pay for.

Everything else in the listing page is self-explanatory. There are also links next to each heading on the listing page, in case you do not understand something.

Two of the most important things to consider when building an auction are the item's title and the cover photograph. These are what potential bidders use to determine whether they are going to click on your auction and hopefully bid on your item. Ensure that your image is clear and you can tell what the item is. Remember, the image boxes are fairly small on the EBay auctions pages. Also, anything that makes your image stand out is helpful. Make your photo as colorful or distinct as possible. If your item is not very exciting, you may decide to give your item a colorful backdrop or background.

The item's title should also accurately and completely describe it, without sounding "over-the-top". Make sure that you include brand names and dates if you know them. With books, make sure that you have the title, author, and edition number.

In the item description, describe the condition of the item as accurately as possible. Do not try to make your item sound better than it is so that you can make a couple of extra dollars on it. Also, list any other description detractions that are not visible in the photographs that you provided.

List your item. When the auction ends in seven days (unless you specified fewer days), EBay notifies the winning bidder by e-mail that they have won your auction. Payment is made through PayPal, and then you are notified, along with the winner's shipping information.

Securely package the item, and ship to the address provided. It is as easy as that.

Another very easy website to sell on is Amazon. If the item that you want to sell is a media item or has a bar code, it is probably available to sell on Amazon. Selling on Amazon is extremely fast and easy. It is also profitable.

All you have to do to sell on Amazon is open a selling account. You will have to provide a checking or savings account for Amazon to deposit your money into, but it is a huge secure marketplace with thousands of sellers. Don't worry about providing your financial information.

Before signing up, determine how many items you will be selling on the site. When you get to the point that you will be consistently selling at least 40 individual items a month on Amazon, you should upgrade to a premium sellers account. The upgraded account eliminates a $1 fee that is charged on each item sold for sellers with a normal seller account. It also allows you to sell some items that normal sellers cannot, and you can also make your own item pages, which I use regularly for selling rare collectible items. The price for the premium account is currently $39.95.

To list your items on Amazon, all you have to do is locate the item within the marketplace by doing a search for that item. For instance, if you wanted to sell a copy of the Nirvana 'Nevermind' CD, you would search for it in the 'Music' category. You can either type in 'Nirvana Nevermind' into the search bar at the top of the page, or if you have the CD in hand, you can type in the bar code number on the back of the CD. It is always found below the bar code, and includes the smaller numbers at the beginning and end of the bar code. For U.S. items, the bar code has 10 numbers, and for European items, there are 13 numbers.

For books and media items, there is usually an ISBN number provided on the title page or on the item cover that you can type in.

When you find the correct item page, there is a link that says 'Sell Your Item' on the right side of the page. You click on that button, and then simply type in your description of the condition of the item, enter your asking price, and then click 'complete', and your item is for sale on Amazon. It is very quick and easy.

When a potential buyer goes to the Nirvana 'Nevermind' page to buy the CD, they see a number of individual listings for that CD, along with your listing. The buyer chooses the copy that they want to buy, based on the price and condition description provided. The buyer clicks 'buy' to complete the sale. There is no bidding, as on eBay.

You do not have to take photographs for your item, or making time consuming listings. If the buyer picks your item, Amazon takes a closing fee from your selling price, gives you a shipping credit and then deposits the balance into your account.

When you get enough money in your Amazon balance, you can then deposit it directly into your personal bank account, or Amazon does it automatically for you every two weeks.

You can see that there are advantages to selling on Amazon versus eBay. First, it is much easier and faster to list items. A box full of CDs can be listed in about a half an hour on Amazon. It is also free to list items. You don't get charged until someone buys your item through the Amazon marketplace. You can build an inventory without any upfront cost. On eBay, you are charged a listing fee for each individual auction listed, whether the item sells at auction, or ends without a bid.

Amazon can be a catch-22 proposition for selling items, in that you may sell your item the same day you list it for more than you can sell it for at auction on EBay. However, you could also list a great $100 collectible book on Amazon, and it may sit there on your shelf for over a year before the right buyer comes along and buys it from you, or it may never sell at all.

You are also constantly competing with other sellers' prices listed on Amazon. You could have the only copy of a collectible item available on the Amazon marketplace for months for $250, and then have another Amazon seller list the same item for significantly less than your price, and then steal your sale when it is purchased several days later from that other seller.

Amazon also charges what I would consider exorbitant selling fees when your item sells; significantly higher than eBay's closing and listing fees combined. Amazon knows that they have very little competition in their niche, and they take advantage of that.

The seller has a number of things to weigh when determining where to sell online. How quickly do you want your money? Do you have room to store items for a period of time? Is it more important for you to maximize profit per item, or sell items fast for a bit less money? Is your item collectible and therefore may do better on EBay, where bidders can see photos of your cool looking item, and also let you tell them about the item in your description?

There are also other places to sell online, and after you determine your own niche, you may decide to build a website, but to begin with, eBay and Amazon are the two easiest online sites to begin selling on.

There are also many physical stores that you can sell items to. Collectible items can be sold to stores that specialize in selling collectibles, such as sports collectibles shops. They can also be sold to pawn shops, antique stores, etc. The most important thing about selling your item to these people is YOU HAVE TO KNOW HOW MUCH YOUR ITEM IS WORTH BEFORE you go the store to sell it. Period. Do your research online and find current values for commodities with spot prices, like gold and silver items, or search completed listings on eBay for similar items. Do NOT allow a pawn shop owner to swindle you. You have to realize that while you will get cash in hand at these types of places, you will not get full value for your items. The shop owner has to make a profit when he or she sells your item again. You will almost always get more for your item online than at a physical store. You have to weigh ease of selling and immediate sales against maximum profit and more prep time selling online.

WHERE TO FIND ITEMS TO SELL

It is surprisingly easy to find cheap stuff to sell. It is all around you, and you probably don't even know it.

Let's start with your home. Hopefully, somebody at your house is a pack-rat and you haven't had a garage sale in several years. Here is the most important thing to remember. Almost everything has a value to somebody. You just have to find that person or group of people to sell your stuff to.

Start looking around your house, and then look again. The second time, try to see your belongings through a collector's eyes. Do you have any old toys that are collectible? How about old biker's jackets, vintage T-shirts or retro dresses. All of this stuff is collectible. Do you have old books or comics? What about your old collection of marbles, baseball cards, or buttons? These are all collectible. What about that old box of stuff your uncle gave you with his old racing trophies and the broken Commodore 64 computer in it? Yep. Collectible.

Once you start looking, you will be surprised what people collect. Old playing cards, yes. Matchbooks, yes. Beer caps and cans. Yes. Just start gathering stuff that you look at and say, hmm... maybe somebody collects this. If somebody ever thought that the item was cool, I will guarantee you that somebody still thinks it is cool today, and therefore worth money. I will show you how to determine value later.

Another place you can make some quick money is with non-functional electronics and appliances. If it's been broken for a long time, it may very well be collectible and worth fixing now.

Several years ago, I found a Simon electronic game in a 'Free' box in a garage sale. I grabbed it and brought it home. It didn't work, so I opened the battery compartment. It only needed to have the terminals cleaned, and it worked like new. I sold it in a week for $50. It is amazing how often broken stuff can be fixed for free and with very little effort.

Also, high-end equipment can be sold for parts, even if it is not repairable. For instance, the cushioned feet on high-end audio equipment can sell for $25, and that's just for the feet.

Many of the components can be sold on EBay, even if the item hasn't worked in years! You can also scrap larger appliances for scrap value. Junk computers may have $20 or more in scrap gold, silver, and copper inside them, as well as having usable components that you can sell separately. The trick is to find where on EBay to sell the scrap and parts.

If you are willing to do some work, you can even scrap whole vehicles and sell many of the resulting parts on EBay. Then, you can scrap the remaining steel auto body for up to $250 at a scrap yard.

Do you have any decaying cars, snowmobiles, or lawnmowers in your yard or pole barn? Have any 25 year old bikes in your garage? They are probably worth at least $50 apiece. You can see where I'm going here. Check the list at the end of the book for more ideas about things to look for.

The bottom line is, if you have something that you can sell at a garage sale, you can probably sell it for considerably more on eBay.

Now that you have cleared out your collectibles, move on to clothing. Vintage clothing should be sold individually. Many jackets, headwear, suits, ties, shoes, dresses, etc. can sell for more than what you would think on EBay. Next, gather your clothing that is in good shape, but you don't wear anymore, or the kids have outgrown. You can sell clothes lots on EBay for a good profit, or you can take them to a second-hand store and set up an account and have them sell clothes for you there. You get a percentage of each sale. Take your remaining clothes and put them in your Goodwill box. Keep track of what's in the box, because you will be writing the value off on your income taxes.

Next, if you have kids, gather all of their toys and games that they have outgrown or don't play with. Check Amazon first. I was amazed by what I have been able sell used toys for on Amazon. It the toy has a box with a bar code, it's very easy to find and sell them. Simply type in the numbers under the bar code into the Amazon search bar.

Even toys without boxes can be sold by searching for the name of the toy. This is true even of smaller Tonka toys, action figures, baby toys, etc. It sometimes takes a while to sell, but they often sell for a lot more than on eBay. Board games can sell very well on Amazon, too, but toys can sometimes take a long time to get off your shelves.

What you don't list on Amazon, check on eBay. If your toy or groups of toys have sold well on EBay in completed listings, make a listing and sell them. Remember to always check discarded toys for usable batteries before listing them or getting rid of them. Batteries are expensive! They also add to the shipping weight, and should not be shipped inside of toys or electronics for fear of the batteries leaking and causing damage.

OK. All of the toys that have not been listed on Amazon and EBay can be put in a box. Cut off anything with a copper wire or brass pieces and save them. Look and see if there is anything worth disassembling for parts. Tip: I have sold battery compartment covers, cases from electronic games, board game pieces, and lots of other parts that are easily broken or lost on eBay for good money.

Everything that can't be sold or scrapped should go in the Goodwill box. Write down all of the toys in the box for your taxes.

Next go to your storage areas, closets and attic. Go through all of your junk boxes. Take out everything that might be collectible and check values in EBay completed listings. Most any everyday item that is usable and in good condition can also be sold on EBay. Put all of your electronics and appliances in one area. If they work, check completed listings and see if they have value on EBay. If they do have value, sell them. If they don't, scrap them for metal value.

Keep metals separated, especially copper and brass. Many scrap dealers will also buy electronics by the pound for scrap value. You can sell the electric motors inside of electronics, as well as any parts containing solid copper (not wires) as 'copper breakage' for good money. I will provide you with a sample list from a scrap dealer that shows how to scrap appliances and what you can get per pound for the pieces.

Check all of your home décor items (knick-knacks, curios) on EBay to see if they are worth selling there. Many have decent value. Some you can group together in a lot (Hallmark ornaments, collectible plates, bells, etc.). If you have anything that looks like it is made of brass or is copper colored, check them with a magnet. If they don't stick to a magnet, they are pure copper or brass and should be sold as such. Currently, spot price for copper is over $3 a pound and brass is over $2 a pound. You can either save these metals for scrap value, or sell on EBay if you think you can make more than the spot price per pound. If you have high value items like Longaberger baskets, nice antiques, or Hummel figurines, make sure you know what they are worth before listing them, or have them appraised. They can be worth big bucks.

Now go to the garage or tool shed. Take any power tool that you don't use and see if it works. If it does, and there is value on EBay, sell it there. Most power tools sell well on EBay. If it does not have value and the tool has a rechargeable battery, the batteries are often worth as much as the used sale price of the whole tool, if the battery has good life left. The battery charger should also be sold with the battery, or separately if the battery is dead.

Hand tools can be sold in lots or individually, in some cases. Everything left that is made of metal, put in your scrap metal pile. Anything electric that doesn't work should at least have the power cord cut off for copper scrap. Heavier items should be disassembled for copper breakage and other scrap value. Check anything that contains a battery to see if the batteries or battery holders are usable or sellable.

We have completed the home sweep. You probably found a bunch of other sellable stuff that I did not even mention, once you got searching. You now also know where to look for good stuff in your relatives and friends homes. Most of the time they will give you this stuff for free, especially if you are willing to do some work and clean up the boxes and other stuff lying around their homes for them.

Additionally, metals like copper, non-magnetic aluminum and brass can be easily collected in a small box by your family and friends, and then you can pick up the boxes periodically when you visit them. Perhaps you feel generous, and decide to give them a little cash for their trouble.

Once you have practiced at home, you will come up with all sorts of places to find similar items for cheap. Sellers at garage sales, second-hand stores, Salvation Armies, Goodwill Stores and flea markets often have not done their homework on what they have for sale, and you can get high-end items for under a dollar, especially at garage sales.

Check the road-sides for free metal, especially anything with a power cord.

FINDING INVENTORY ONLINE

There are also numerous places to find items to sell online. Finding items from your computer or portable device can be particularly advantageous if you are tied to a desk at work or only have time to look for inventory when most physical stores are closed.

Bargains abound on eBay and Craigslist, but you have to consider that you are competing with other resellers for your items to sell, and it will cost you more to get your source material to sell than it would if you found the same item at a garage sale. You also have to consider that on top of the higher cost per item, you will also probably have to pay shipping costs for your items.

Having said that, there is definitely profit to be made on many items listed on eBay. So... What are we looking for exactly, you ask? The trick is to be smarter and more diligent than your competing sellers on EBay. You want to win your items for the lowest possible ending price (net ending price, including shipping costs).

I have had very good luck winning large lots of items, such as boxes of books, and then re-listing individual books from the lots on eBay or Amazon. I have found several $100 books and quite a few $50 collectible books in bulk lots of books that I won for under $5. I have also won quite a few books and other collectibles for 99 cents, which I immediately re-listed with a better listing page and resold for over $50.

Here are some quick pointers. Do not bid until the last minute of an online auction if at all possible. Many auctions do not get bids at all, especially obscure collectibles that are valuable only to a select few. These items can be very profitable, if you have the ability to find those people that collect them. You may have to re-list these items multiple times, or allow them to sit in your Amazon inventory for months. But, they have the potential to make big profits.

Items that do have bids tend to draw the competition's attention, and if you bid early, someone will often outbid you at the last second. There are 'auction sniping' programs and applications that can help you win bids at the very last second, but they cost money. It's up to you to determine if you think the program is worth the added expense.

Look for inventory when you don't have a lot of competing bidders. You can steal auctions late at night, on holidays, and early in the morning.

You are also looking for the lazy sellers' auction items or lots. Try to find the lots where the listing seller did not do his or her homework and does not know the value of the items. Look for misspelled words and author's or musician's names.

Look for short descriptions that don't specify content. For instance, an EBay listing titled only 'Grammas old books' would definitely catch my attention for several reasons. Number one, the books are probably going to be older and potentially collectible. Number two, the seller is lazy and not very bright. They cannot spell 'grandma', and they didn't care enough to tell the bidders what kind of books are in the lot and whether they were valuable.

I typically search specific category locations where bulk lots are listed like music, books, or collectibles. You are given check boxes on the top of the page that allows you to sort by 'best match', 'lowest price', etc. I click on 'lowest price, plus shipping', which gives you the entire category listed, with the lowest priced items, plus shipping costs added in at the top.

Usually you have to sift through a bunch of garbage for the first couple of pages, but sometimes you will find a gem. You can also sort by auctions 'Ending Soonest' to see the auctions that are very close to ending. That can also help you win excellent lots or items.

When I find interesting auctions to bid on, I 'Watch' the auctions. Watching auctions allows you to easily come back to the auction at a later date or time if the price at the end of the auction is still to your liking.

Simply go to your 'My EBay' page, click on your 'Bidding' link and check the auctions that you are watching. If you are watching a number of items, you should leave yourself a note somewhere where you will see it often, reminding you of what the item is, when it ends, and how high you are willing to bid to win the auction. It's easy to get tied up with something else and miss the end of an auction that you really wanted to win without placing a bid.

Another idea is to search for a specific title, instead of looking in your usual categories. A lot of times, sellers will accidentally list items in the wrong category by forgetting to change the category when they are listing many auctions at once (Yes, I've done it, too.). Some sellers just do not know where to sell items, and list them in the wrong locations, as well.

There are additional considerations with EBay auctions. Don't get burned by a lazy or dishonest seller. EBay provides bidders with information to avoid some of these problems. After a person wins an auction and receives the item that they won, they are given an opportunity to provide 'feedback' to other potential bidders, regarding their buying experience for that particular seller.

Each seller is given a feedback score that tells you how many feedbacks they have received. It also has a positive feedback percentage to the right of the seller's name. If the seller has had over 100 feedbacks, and a score of over 95%, they are probably a reliable seller. You can also read individual feedbacks by clicking on the feedback number, and you can read what other buyers had to say about their experience with that seller.

You also want to CAREFULLY read the descriptions of the items that you are potentially bidding on, and make sure that you understand what the seller is listing. It seems like that would be obvious, but quite often, sellers don't take the time to adequately describe items. Sometimes, they just don't have time because they are listing tons of items. Other times, items have short descriptions in order to purposefully omit condition issues with the item(s).

Make sure that you have the information you need BEFORE bidding on it, especially if the auction would potentially cost you some money. Use the 'Ask Seller' link to get the information you need before you place a bid.

THE BOTTOM LINE ON EBAY BUYING

Here is my secret formula to successful eBay bidding. I locate items to bid on, and do not bid early, as we have already discussed. When I am looking for items, I use at least two browser tabs. One is for the eBay listings I am searching.

I also have a second tab open to check the value of items. For media items, I use Amazon. It is very easy to search for items in the Amazon marketplace and look at the average price listed for items within the lots that you are looking for during your eBay search. AdAll.com is another location to find values for rare collectible books.

If I am searching in collectibles or other eBay categories, I open a second browser tab for searching Completed eBay Listings. I search for the item on the first tab, and then look at the ending prices for similar auctions over the last three months on the second tab.

I generally do not get overly excited about an auction unless I know that there are several individual items that are valuable within the lot. I do not like guessing what items may be hidden in an auction lot. Usually, you can see enough either in the text of the auction's description or by looking at the photographs provided to tell if the lot is worth your time. Watch out for the sneaky seller who sells a large lot of garbage and then throws in one or two valuable items to attract bids. If you only see one or two photos of nice items, but no pictures of the overall lot, or a detailed description of what's in there, look out!

If I can verify that several of the items within the lot will pay for the entire cost of the auction, including shipping, I attempt to win the auction. After a while, you get pretty good at getting a feel for which auctions will also have extra hidden goodies in the lot, besides what was listed or photographed.

It's always fun opening your large boxes of goodies to see what you got. Sometimes, you'll have over $100 in extra inventory that you didn't even know about inside your package. Sometimes you only get what was listed in the auction, but, if you did your homework, you should always come out ahead when you re-list the individual items. Plus, you can re-list the remainder of the items that had little value as a lot on eBay, sell it at a garage sale, or donate it to Goodwill for a tax write-off.

GARAGE SALES SHOPPING

Finding stuff to make large profits on at garage sales used to be easy. Now, there are many people re-selling items from garage sales on eBay. Plus, the people holding the garage sales are more aware of the value of many collectible items than they used to be, so items are often priced higher. Still, you can find a lot of great items to sell at sales, often for very cheap prices. You can regularly find $10-20 items for under a dollar. How's that for profit?

Here are a number of tips to help you find stuff at garage sales to sell. Number one, do your homework ahead of time. Go through the newspaper classifieds and Craigslist to find sales that advertise what you like to sell, or similar items. Write down when the sales start and end, and what they are supposed to have at the sale that you are interested in. Look for sales that advertise large bunches of stuff, '25 years of accumulation', or that type of language in the ad.

Make every effort to be at the most attractive sale first when it opens. If you can go to sales on Thursdays and Fridays, you can find much more material to sell than if you wait until the sale has been running for a day or two on Saturday morning. Make yourself a route that hits all of the good sales. This prevents you from wasting time and gas money by going back and forth across the county to get to all of the garage sales. If you can hit a neighborhood or citywide sale, by all means, go there.

Number two, don't waste time fiddle-farting around at sales. Treat your garage sailing as a business. It is fun to find stuff at sales, but you are there for a reason. Say hello to the homeowner and be polite, but don't talk for half an hour. If you get to the tables, and there is obviously only junk there, leave immediately and move on to the next one.

If you do find items that you want to buy, ask if you can stack them by the pay table. Get what you are going to get at the sale, pay, and leave. This allows you to hit the most sales possible in the time that you have for that day.

Number three, look at EVERYTHING at the sale. This may seem to contradict rule number two at first glance, but it really does not. When you get more experienced hitting sales, you will understand exactly what I mean. Don't waste time gabbing, and wandering around, but make sure you look at all the tables at the sale. I have found tons of great items underneath junk on tables, inside other boxes, scattered in amongst books, in boxes of toys, and everywhere else you can think of. The items you are looking for are items that the seller does NOT know the value of. This stuff could be anywhere at the sale.

As a matter of fact, I have found some of my best items in FREE boxes or 5 or 10 cent boxes, thrown in with a bunch of crud. If you see these types of boxes ALWAYS look in them all the way to the bottom of the box. If it's a free box, you can always grab the whole box to save time, and go through it later. You are doing the homeowner a favor by getting rid of the box of junk for them. Take almost any books, CDs, DVDs, or media items that you see in a free box. I have found multiple $50 books in free boxes at sales.

As a savvy reseller, you also have the advantage of having an Amazon selling account. This puts you ahead of 95% of the re-sellers you are competing with at garage sales, who are only selling on eBay. Look for media items that you can sell for a higher price on Amazon, as well as boxed items with bar codes that you can resell. Make sure you quickly grab anything sealed in shrink wrap that you can sell as 'New'.

Number four may be the most important rule. Make sure that you can sell the items that you are picking up. Condition of the item is one of the most important things to consider when deciding on whether to buy an item. Is the item operational? Does it have all the parts? Does it need additional cords to be usable?

Plug electronic items in to test them. Almost everybody has outdoor outlets available to test with. If they refuse to let you test an item, don't buy it. It probably does not work.

Also, keep in mind that some items are valuable without being functional. You just have to remember that you are going to have to spend additional money for parts, plus spend time fixing the item, which cuts into your profit.

For instance, it is quite common to find video game systems without cords. That does not mean that you should not buy them if the price is right. It is very easy to get cords online for any video game system, and they are usually fairly cheap. You can also save the systems for a while and try to find cords at other sales, or at second-hand stores.

Make sure you examine the entire item. Does it have broken corners, re-glued pieces, etc.? If it does, the collectible value is going to be significantly reduced.

Also, keep in mind the shipping cost of heavy items. There are many collectible items that would make nice profits, if it was not for the weight of the item. Figure on all items over one pound to cost over $5 in shipping costs, plus an extra $2+ for every pound after that. A heavy metal item could easy cost your potential winning bidder on eBay an additional $15 in shipping fees on top of their winning bid. Consider the total cost that you think the average collector would pay for an item.

Let's say you found a really cool retro glass lamp that is priced $5 at a garage sale.

From your prior research, you have seen comparable lamps priced at about $25 at antique stores. Should you buy this lamp, if it appears operational?

The answer is: You probably will not make much profit on this lamp. The antique shop owner may offer you a slight profit over the $5 that you would be paying for it, but by the time you figure your drive time to the antique store, you won't make much money there. If you planned on selling the lamp online, remember that the lamp weighs over ten pounds and would cost the potential buyer $15-20 in shipping fees over top of their winning bid.

Large items are also a pain to package, and you have to pay for bubble wrap to prevent damage. So, while the lamp looked like a great item at the garage sale, it probably would be a break-even venture for you in the long run.

Number five, keep a magnet in your pocket for identifying valuable scrap metals such as copper, brass, and silver-plate. Remember that non-magnetic metals are usually more valuable than the metal objects that stick to your magnet.

RESEARCHING

If there is one area that a motivated seller will stand out above their competition, it is in their knowledge base pertaining to the items they sell. If I could give you one piece of advice, it would be this: Start with what you know, and then broaden your knowledge from there.

You really do not have to know much to sell usable items, clothing, and other non-collectible items online. You simply identify the item in an auction or on the Amazon marketplace, describe the condition, and then make it available for purchase.

However, other items such as collectibles, high-end electronics, computer equipment, and auto parts require the seller to have some background knowledge before selling the item. In order to be able to describe the item sufficiently so that a potential buyer is comfortable buying it from you, the seller has to understand what type of information the buyer needs for them to determine value and functionality.

Start selling what you are familiar with. If you grew up collecting sports cards and memorabilia, and you have boxes of baseball cards in your closet, start by selling your excess cards. You already know how to describe your cards to buyers. You can 'speak the language' to collectors on eBay. You know what an insert card is, and how to identify a rookie card. You know how to describe the condition of the card to a potential buyer.

Get yourself a current price guide for your sports cards so that you have an idea of the current market value. Then, collect a number of cards that you are interested in selling and type the player's name and year of the sport card in the search bar on eBay. Click on the checkbox on the left side of the screen that says 'Completed Listings'. You get a list of the ended auctions from the last three months with your search description. The average ending price is what you should expect to sell your card for, if the condition is also similar.

The same process can be applied to any subject area. When you have an item that you want to determine value on, take a look at the last three months of sales on eBay. You should be able to make a quick determination if the item is worth your time. If you are considering selling the item on Amazon, locate the item in the Amazon marketplace using the search bar, and see what the average price listed is.

EBay completed listings can also help you in other ways. Let's say that you found a vintage Pioneer audio receiver for free at a garage sale. Good for you! Now, how do you make a profit on it, if you have never dealt with electronics before?

If you plug it in and everything works, you just hit the jackpot. Look on the back of the unit and find the model number. Type it into the search bar, and see what similar working units have sold for, and list your receiver starting at the low end of the completed listing's end prices. You want to encourage bidders by starting at what feels like a bargain to the bidder.

If you attempt to test the receiver and it doesn't work at all, don't fret. You actually may make more money by disassembling the receiver and selling the parts.

The trick is to determine which components and parts to sell. You should have an idea what parts are going to be sold BEFORE taking the receiver apart, because some larger components are more valuable whole then totally disassembled. For instance, if your vintage audio item has a record player, you will want to keep the entire tone-arm assembly together to sell it.

In order to determine what we are going to sell, we use Completed Listings again. Type in the model number from the receiver on the main eBay page. Most of the time, the search will return many whole receivers that were for sale. But, it will also give you a list of parts and components that other sellers have listed and what the ending prices were.

For instance, with vintage Pioneer receivers, you would probably find that the outer case was worth listing (and would make you some good money, if it was wood). You would also note that the knobs, feet, emblem, and face plate were worth money. Usually the tuning mechanism, display, and some of the internal workings will also be listed.

You may also want to go to the 'Vintage Electronics' category and look at the Completed Listings for the entire category. This will give you a general idea of some of the parts that are often valuable, regardless of brand. You would probably note that large power transformers are usually worth money, and since your Pioneer has a similar transformer to the ones that you saw in Completed Listings, you would want to list your own transformer in the category that you found the others in.

A good seller is curious. If you are at a garage sale, you should be looking for new sources of income. If you find something interesting, look it up in Completed Listings when you get home, and see if it's worth your time.

I spend a lot of time just browsing Completed Listings in given categories and looking for new areas to list items in. If I find an interesting listing that did really well for another seller, I look at the auction page and try to figure out why it did better than others in the same category. Were there certain words used in the item title? Were the photos showing a certain aspect of the item? Was the item described in a particular way? If I can pick up anything useful, I use similar wordings in my titles or descriptions.

You may also find totally new areas to sell items in. I remember one night browsing Completed Listings to see if any 1980s-era magazines were worth buying at garage sales, because I was seeing them quite often. I found that 95% of the magazines I was seeing were not going to be worth the time it took to list them. But, I saw some listings in other categories that *were* interesting.

Other sellers were listing just the advertisements from magazines and newspapers for pretty decent money. Often, the magazines the ads came from could be found for $1, but the ads within could be worth up to $20 apiece. People were looking for ads containing celebrities or certain products (like vintage autos, or Atari 2600 games) and framing them for décor in their homes and businesses.

So I picked up a bunch of magazines, and clipped interesting ads out. I scanned the ads with my scanner, and listed them on eBay. I made several hundred dollars selling magazine ads in a relatively short time. I looked at a number of sellers' listings, and it was apparent that they sold only magazine ads and did quite well.

I sold ads for a while, but I quickly realized that you have to make a lot of listings to make any real money, and I found it quite monotonous clipping and scanning, so I moved on to more interesting ventures. If you are interested in selling ads, there are books available on Amazon for identifying and pricing print ads to get you started. The startup cost is almost zero, and you will make some money if you can find some older magazines to pull ads from.

FREE ITEMS TO SELL: OUTDOORS

DISCLAIMER: Consult the appropriate laws on the collection of goods and materials from government-owned public lands, whether the lands are federal, state, or municipally owned.

There are often laws pertaining to the commercial use of these lands, and the taking and/or use of wild animals, plants, and minerals or their parts may be restricted or forbidden. Vehicle access may also be restricted to certain areas. You can be fined or possibly even arrested for the violation of these laws, so conduct research on the laws BEFORE you enter these lands.

There are thousands of different things that you can find while you are outside doing yard work, recreating, or bee-bopping around in your ORV, snowmobile, or vehicle that you can quickly and easily sell. While you are out having fun, you might as well try to pay for the gas you put in the gas tank to get you out there, right?

Before you leave your house, you should prepare for locating items to sell. Put together a 'gathering kit' that you can bring with you, whether you are in a car or on a smaller recreational vehicle. Find a small gear bag or backpack that is the right size for you to carry, and does not get in the way of the other activities that you got you outside in the first place.

Inside the bag, you will need a lightweight set of tools that you will use often while gathering items to sell. You will want to tailor your set to the types of items that you like to sell. Make sure that you have plenty of room left over inside the bag to place items when you find them.

At the minimum, I would recommend including the following items: Work gloves, bug spray, a small first aid kit, a small magnet, a multi-tool (Leatherman-type) that has both types of screwdrivers, a knife, needle-nose pliers, and a wire cutter; several additional rolled bags i.e. garbage bags or burlap sacks to put stuff in, a map of the area you are exploring, a compass, a cellular telephone, pencil and paper, and this handy-dandy book for reference.

If you have a handheld GPS or smart-phone that has GPS capabilities, you are ahead of the game. You can mark locations to return to, and easily find your way back to your vehicle if you are out on foot.

OK, so after you are mobile, what are you looking for? Basically anything that people might want to use, or that you can find value in. You have already done part of your research by reading this book. You have an excellent selection of items to look for.

Now, just start thinking logically while you are out having fun. When you see things in the woods, either collect them, or write them down on your pad of paper to check when you get home.

When I started this gig, I sat down in front of a computer and just started searching for things that I could possibly find in the woods in my area. I did searches on EBay completed items and Google searches for items I was seeing while hunting, fishing, or whatever else got me outside. Some items were worth gathering, and some were not. Some items I immediately found that I could sell on eBay, some took more digging to find places to sell them.

ORGANIC ITEMS

I remember duck hunting near an abandoned beaver dam, and seeing lots of cool looking beaver-chewed sticks. I wondered if people would use them for rustic home or cabin décor. I grabbed a couple of medium sized logs with nice wood grains, and took them home. I found several areas on eBay where people had sold similar items for décor and animal taxidermy backgrounds.

People were also using natural beaver logs with no preparation for crafting candle holders for $2-5 apiece. If you wanted to do some work and either make the candle holders yourself, or power-wash and stain the logs, you could make even more money on each item.

In many areas, local businesses will also pay you to bring them outdoor goods and edible items. Bakeries, delicatessens, restaurants, and specialty shops like organic foods stores may pay good money for things you can easily find and gather such as: Berries, nuts, mushrooms, and edible plants like wild asparagus and wild leeks.

If you own wooded property, timber companies may pay you very good money to come to your property and harvest timber. Most timber companies will even do select cutting, where only specific trees are cut, or a stand of trees is thinned. Such a timber harvest is actually very beneficial to the health of the forest and the animals that live there, and any damage to the ground heals naturally in a short time period. Plus, you can receive substantial money for allowing the timber company to harvest on your property.

Similarly, if you own a large tract of land, you may consider contacting an oil and gas company to test your property for mineral harvest. You may be sitting on a gold mine, and don't even know it!

On a smaller scale, many other forest products can be sold to local companies for their resale. Such items would include: Christmas trees, saplings for tree sales, seeds and seed-bearing cones to nurseries for tree regeneration, pine and cedar boughs for wreath making, wood mulch, wood chips, and tree bolts to landscaping companies, and the list goes on and on.

I know several people who make hundreds of dollars every year gathering acorns and other seeds and selling them to tree nurseries, with very little preparation time. You only have to do a little leg work ahead of time and establish a relationship with the managers or owners of these nurseries so that you know what they are buying, and when to bring them your supply to get paid.

MAN-MADE ITEMS

If there is one thing that aggravates me to no end, it is seeing litter in the woods. There should be automatic jail time handed out to any person convicted of littering.

But, there *is* some nice money to be made on trash found in the woods, or along the roadways. I regularly pick up trash when I find it in the woods or in rivers while I'm recreating. While I'm doing my good deed for the day, I'm also going to see if I can make some money on it, as long as I'm spending my time picking up after others.

First of all, make sure that you wear thick work gloves while handling any man-made materials that you find. There is the potential to be seriously cut, and you could contract a number of diseases by being cut by unclean glass or metal.

I do not open any trash bags found in the woods, and I highly recommend that you do not open any closed bags, either. The health concerns are obvious. You don't know what is in the bag, correct? At the least, you could be dealing with rotten food and diapers. At worst, the contents of a garbage bag could be explosive, if a drug manufacturer threw out the remains of a mobile meth lab!

So, where is the value in discarded litter? You should immediately recognize the intrinsic value of picking up unsightly, environmentally degrading litter in the area where you live. It should make you feel proud to help your community and conserve your local environment by making the effort to pick up that litter. That is the value in picking up most plastics, trash bags, broken glass, shingles, and other litter that has no resale value.

It should not be difficult at all to find a local business or a governmental agency that will allow you to dispose of bags of litter that you selflessly picked up from public land. You should not have to pay to dispose of such materials yourself.

There is also a lot of tangible money to be made at these dump sites. I can guarantee you that if 'push came to shove', I could feed my family for months solely off the scrap metal value of litter piles found in the woods on state land where I live. That's not my first choice of material to sell, but it would do just fine in a pinch.

In order to maximize your profit on this scrap metal, consult the chapter on Scrap Metal in this book for the separation and identification of particular metals.

If you have a scrap metal vehicle or trailer, you can continue to add magnetic steel from a number of litter locations until you get a full load to sell at the scrap yard. If you do not have a designated vehicle, you may opt to mark scrap metal spots on a map or GPS unit, until you think that you would have enough steel to make a load, and then pick them all up in the same trip.

Remember to remove anything that is not magnetic (non-ferrous) from the scrap metal, before going to the scrap dealer. Anything that is non-ferrous should be sold separately as it is has significantly more value than ferrous steel.

And now, let's talk about the real money. As you are loading your scrap metal, remove any items with dedicated recyclable value. One example would be aluminum beverage cans in states with deposit laws. There are also many other items with designated values listed in APPENDIX C, such as cellular telephones, Lithium-Ion Batteries, and printer cartridges.

Next, look to see if there is anything that you can sell individually. Look for any media items, like music CDs, DVDs, video games and books that are in good enough shape to sell.

One of my best finds ever was in a trash pile along a road on state land. I stopped to pick up the litter, and noticed a huge pile of 1980s heavy metal CDs that had been tossed out with the litter. Many of the cases and paperwork therein were destroyed by the elements, but 90% of the CDs themselves were just fine.

I listed over 100 of the CDs on Amazon, with values of up to $20 each. I sold most of them within two months! There was also a working video game system worth $50 in the pile. Of course, I also disposed of the rest of the litter that was there. Intrinsic value, folks.

You should also look for board games, handheld video games, and electronics to sell for parts, collectibles, vintage bottles, batteries, battery chargers, computers, cords, remote controls, and other similar items.

Check inside anything with a battery compartment for batteries. I have found many usable alkaline batteries lying around inside litter piles. You can also save the battery compartment doors to sell on commonly owned items like remote controls and toys. Save any rechargeable batteries as well. You can make very good money on large rechargeable batteries, if they are not completely dead. Even if you don't have the manufactured charger, it is still possible to recharge most batteries. I will provide you with a link later in this document that provides directions on how to recharge many supposedly 'dead' batteries.

After you have removed all of the items that you can sell individually and the recyclable items, hit all of the metal with your magnet. Take anything out of the pile that is non- ferrous. Make sure you remove any copper wires and cords. Make a separate pile for this material, or put it in a large sturdy bag. Also include in this pile any junk electronics that you plan on disassembling for sellable parts, or the interior copper and precious metals content.

Finally, remove the large steel frames from any furniture that is there. Items like sleeper sofas can have $10-15 in steel in their frames alone. Put the remaining ferrous metal in your scrap vehicle, separate from your non-ferrous pile. Take your valuable non-ferrous pile, bag it, and remove it. Complete your work by bagging the rest of the litter and disposing of it on the way to scrap metal dealer.

In addition to piles of litter, there are many other free single items that can be found while outside that you can sell. Along roadways you can find hubcaps and wheel rims worth $2-3 each at the scrap metal dealer, recyclable cans, bungee straps, ratchet straps, and if you are really luck, exhaust pipes with the platinum-containing catalytic converters attached. Junk 'Cats' are worth $40-150 each, because of the platinum content inside them!

If you can find a junk vehicle in the woods, congratulations! You can haul the body to the scrap dealer for at least $200, if you can get it out of the woods. If you can't get the car out, you may very well be able to strip out a bunch of parts to sell individually on eBay. You can also remove the 'cat' from newer vehicles, take all of the copper wires, remove the radio, etc. If it is an older vehicle and not too rusted, you may be able to sell the chrome trim, decals, hood ornaments and other collectible items for very good money.

Some other man-made items that I have found and sold or converted to personal use while outdoors are: vintage fishing lures and tackle, golf clubs, golf balls, railroad ties, railroad spikes, lumber, automobile batteries (why would you throw these out? You get at least $5 just by taking them to Wal-Mart!), tools, doors, door knobs, bench seats, coolers, bottles, vintage cans, winter outerwear, a paintball helmet, copper pipes, tents, hunting blinds, ice spuds, duck decoys, duck decoy anchors, shotgun shell hulls, brass shell casings, vintage shotgun shell boxes, can openers, collectible lighters, folding chairs, camp chairs, working radios, Walkman radios, an I-pod, and on and on.

For a complete list of free outdoor items that you can sell and where to sell them, see the Outdoors Items Appendix provided with this document.

SELLING SCRAP METAL: EASIEST MONEY YOU'LL EVER MAKE

I wish I could go back in time. If I could transport myself back to when I was a teenager, with the knowledge I have now about selling scrap metal, I could have saved myself several summers of misery working at the local grocery store. I could have been working outside at my own pace, and made twice as much money as I did bagging groceries and dealing with snobby tourists.

Finding and selling scrap metal is extremely easy, not very competitive, and you can do it anywhere. You can start collecting scrap for free, and you do not need a large area to collect it in. Plus, there is good money to be made in selling scrap.

In addition, you are cleaning up the environment by picking up metal that would otherwise take decades to biodegrade. You are keeping materials that you can make money on from being taken to landfills, and we have all heard that many landfills are completely full already.

So why doesn't everybody sell scrap metal, if it is so easy to make money on? Good question. I think that there are several things that keep the majority of people away. Many people seem to think that you have to be a scientist to identify different types of metals, and that selling to a scrap metal dealer is a mysterious process that requires extensive training to be able to complete.

This could not be further from the truth. You need absolutely no prior knowledge of metals to sell scrap. Selling scrap metal can be as simple as this: Find metal objects, throw them into a truck, transport the metal to the scrap metal dealer, drive your truck onto their scales just as you would pull into a drive-through car wash, unload the metal from your truck where they tell you to, re-weigh your truck, and go into the dealer to get paid. The whole process can be completed in twenty minutes for a pick-up sized load.

It is extremely easy, and you do not even have to know what type of metal you have. Of course, you will make much more money once you know how to separate your metals, but that is easily accomplished, too.

I also think that there is the perception that selling scrap would take up a lot of room on one's property, and that scrapping is a messy business. Well, that may be true if you are a large-scale scrapping outfit, but you can contain a modest scrap metal venture in a very small area.

I got into selling scrap as a way to minimize the loss on metal items that I had bought at garage sales to sell on EBay, but ended up not being able to sell. I was also picking up litter from the woods and looking for someplace to take the metal so that I did not have to throw it in the trash.

Initially, I just started throwing all of the metal into the bed of my plow truck, which I only used in the winter. The first time I emptied the truck out at the scrap metal dealer, I made $160, selling all types of metals together as 'Tin', which is how most scrap metal dealers classify loads of metal that are unprocessed.

Later, I did more research on scrapping, and found out that I could have made an extra $50 by selling the aluminum objects separate from the rest of the load. But hey, I was pretty happy at the time, making $160 on a bunch of junk.

GETTING STARTED SELLING SCRAP METAL

You can start collecting scrap without spending any money at all. All you need is a small area to collect metal in, some large boxes or bins, heavy work gloves, the tool kit described in the Outdoors section of this book, a magnet, and a vehicle or trailer to haul the metal to the scrap dealer in. Bolt cutters and a hacksaw come in handy, as well.

This chapter is intended to be a very general guide to the art of scrapping. After reading this chapter, you should feel very comfortable with the process of selling scrap metal. You will understand the basics of how to separate metal, and where to go online to increase your knowledge base. It is not a complete how-to manual for starting a scrap metal business. You will still need to broaden your knowledge of metals through experience and your own research.

Selling scrap metal is one area in which people with very little spare time can save themselves and their family significant money. Even if you do not want to commit the time and effort into starting a second business using the other information in this book, you should strongly consider selling scrap metal. You could easily save enough metal to sell once a year and pay for all of the Christmas presents for your family!

THE BASICS OF SCRAPPING

You have to realize that the scrap metal business works just like any other business. The metal itself has a value, which is similar to stock prices. The value is called a spot price. The spot price of each particular type of metal fluctuates, depending on supply and demand for that metal across large regions of the country and the world. The spot prices for each type of metal can be found at any time on the internet.

The spot price is the only point in the scrap selling process that has a fixed value. Everything else is determined by individual scrap metal dealers. To illustrate this, let's say that you have a load of shiny aluminum to sell. You check online, and see that the spot price for Aluminum is $0.85/LB. Should you expect to be paid $0.85/LB when you go to your local scrap dealer? Of course not.

The spot price is quoted for clean processed aluminum. You have used manufactured aluminum. The dealer you are selling it to is a middle-man. He has to buy your metal, and then negotiate a better price with the larger metal processing company that he sells to in order to make a profit.

What does that mean for you? Number one, you will never sell your scrap metal at the spot price, but it gives you a good indicator of whether the metal's value is rising or falling. Try to sell when the spot price is rising, not at the bottom of a price fall.

Number two, the prices quoted to you at a scrap metal dealer are not etched in stone and they are not the same at all scrap metal dealers in your area.

Scrap metal pricing is similar to how gas stations set gas prices. Not all of the gas stations in your area will charge the same price for a gallon of unleaded gas, but they will almost always be in the same ball park because of the overriding oil prices.

The difference between metal and gas is that sometimes if you contact the scrap metal dealer ahead of time, the buy price for particular metals can be adjusted if you have a large load of a particular type of metal. At the very least, you may want to check around to see which scrap dealer has the best buy price for the metal you are going to be selling before you decide where to take your scrap.

Before you even start scrapping, you should go to a Metal Spot Price internet page and take a look at the values of the common metals that you will be finding. You should know which metals are more valuable, so that you can look for them.

SEPARATING SCRAP METALS

The easiest way to increase your profits in the scrapping business is to correctly identify and separate the more valuable non-ferrous (non-magnetic) metals from the more commonly found ferrous metals, such as steel.

Let's revisit the load of metal that we sold at the beginning of this chapter. $160 is not bad for a load of junk metal. But, if you are going to make the effort to save the metal and haul it to the scrap dealer, you may as well get the maximum value for it.

You will want to sell loads of one particular classification of metal whenever possible, instead of half-full loads, or mixed metal loads. At the very least, you will want to remove the non-ferrous metal from the steel. Steel will get you about $240 a ton, or about 12 cents a pound. Shiny Aluminum can be sold for over 45 cents a pound, and bare copper wires can be sold for over $2.50 a pound.

Copper and aluminum can often be found inside large metal items, such as appliances. You can usually remove the more valuable metals in several minutes, making it well worth your time to do so.

So how do I tell the different types of metal apart, you may ask. There are many ways to identify metals, but the easiest method to separate metals is to use the visible characteristics of the metals. If the metal is not silver colored, remove it from the rest of the scrap. Non-silver metals would include copper, brass, bronze, gold (if you are lucky), and their alloys. All of these metals are worth removing and collecting separately.

For similarly colored metals, there are several ways to further distinguish them. The first way is to check the metal object with a magnet. This is particularly helpful for separating non-magnetic stainless steel and thick aluminum from common magnetic steel. A magnet will also tell you if a copper colored metal item is pure copper or an alloy, which is worth much less.

Another easy way to separate metals is by their weight. Lead items are extremely dense and very heavy. Steel items are also relatively heavy. Aluminum, on the other hand, is fairly light compared to non-ferrous Stainless steel. Shiny aluminum and non-ferrous Stainless can be difficult to differentiate for beginners.

A third way you can tell metals apart is with a 'spark test'. This method sounds more difficult than the other two methods, but really is quite easy. All it involves is hitting your metal with a rotary tool (Dremel) with a cutting wheel. This is extremely helpful for differentiating stainless steel and thick aluminum. Steel sparks, aluminum does not. You can also identify several high value metal carbides with a spark test.

Once you start separating the different types of metals, you will quickly become proficient at the task, and you will often be able to tell what type of metal an object is made of just by looking at it, or feeling the weight of it.

A TRIP TO THE SCRAP METAL DEALER

As I alluded to earlier, one reason many people do not sell scrap metal is because they are unfamiliar with the process of selling metal to a dealer. I believe that after reading this chapter, you will feel confident enough to go to the scrap dealer on your own for the first time.

I will go over a typical trip to the metal dealer. You will see that there really is nothing difficult about the process. The only thing that is difficult at all is loading the heavy metal into your truck or trailer.

The first thing that you must do is take an inventory of all of your collected scrap metal. Every trip that you make to the scrap yard costs you gas money and time, so minimize the number of trips, if at all possible.

You should already have your metals separated ahead of time. Usually, when I go to the scrap dealer to sell scrap, I have a pickup bed-load of steel. Put as much metal into the bed of you truck as possible, and then use ratchet straps or tie-downs to secure your load. It is illegal to transport large loads without securing them, and it is also dangerous for you and other motorists.

You may also have enough aluminum to fill a small trailer. If so, you can bring the trailer with you and save yourself a trip. Make sure to secure your load, just as you did with the scrap in your truck bed.

I usually have some non-ferrous scrap to sell, as well. That is where the real money is. You can pack up the inside of your vehicle with boxes of copper, brass, small amounts of aluminum, and other separated non-ferrous metals. For those people without access to pickup trucks or trailers, you will probably only be selling non-ferrous metals, as the ferrous metals are not going to be worth your time. You cannot transport enough volume of non-ferrous metal to make the trips worthwhile.

The only thing that you really have to prepare for is the unloading of the metal at the scrap yard. Make sure that you have your non-ferrous separated, and placed in either heavy bags or sturdy boxes, so that it is easy to handle when you unload at the scrap yard.

Before you leave, check all of your tie-downs, check the tires on your vehicle and trailer, and the fluids in your vehicle. You may be hauling more weight than your vehicle is used to, if you do not normally work your vehicles hard. It's OK if your vehicle looks like the truck from the TV show 'Sanford & Son' when you're ready to go. It is not supposed to look pretty.

Make sure that you have a pair of heavy work gloves, work clothes, and possibly a flat shovel for scooping loose metal pieces from your truck or trailer. It also doesn't hurt to have a hammer and crowbar, because sometimes large metal pieces will get wedged together and you will have to separate them.

When you arrive at the scrap yard, there will be an office building with a set of drive-on scales nearby, at the front of the property. Pull off of the road, and go into the office. Make sure that you have your wallet or purse with you.

Go to the main desk, and tell the attendant that you have scrap metal to sell. You will provide your identification, or the attendant may ask you for personal information, address, etc. This information is provided to prevent criminals from illegally selling stolen copper pipes and other high-end metals to scrap yards, and also is used to issue your check when your trip is complete.

The attendant will usually ask you whether you have non-ferrous metals to sell. The attendant will hand you a ticket or sheet of paper with your information on it, and send you back to your vehicle.

If you have non-ferrous metal to sell (which you should), you may be instructed to go to the non-ferrous unloading area first. When you get to the specified location, you will unload your boxes or bags of separated non-ferrous metals one material at a time. Each material will be weighed on a foot scale inside, and then you will deposit the material where the employee tells you to place it. The employee keeps track of the weight of the materials you brought. When you are done dropping off all of your non-ferrous metals, the employee will give his list of weights and materials to the main office for calculation. You may also receive a copy. This process takes only several minutes.

Next, you will sell your ferrous metals, which is usually steel, or mixed metal which is sold as 'Tin', or 'Unprocessed'. Pull your vehicle onto the main scale near the office building. There will be a large metal area on the scale, where you will center the weight of your load. Usually there is a set of lights that resemble traffic lights near the window of the office building.

The attendant inside the office will look out the window at your vehicle. Once it is positioned correctly and the weight from the scale has been recorded, the light will change colors, and you will proceed through the scales and into the main scrap yard.

Usually within sight of the scales, there will be another employee waiting for you. He or she will take a look at your load, and determine what type of material you have for the payment calculation. Hopefully, you have separated your metal, so that your payment is not calculated using the 'unprocessed' rate, as you will be losing significant money.

The employee will make a note on your ticket about the contents of your load, and then he or she will direct you where to dump. If you have all steel, you will be sent to an area where a large magnet will pick up the majority of the metal.

If you have a mixed load, or a bed cap or something else that prevents the magnet from unloading your metal, you will be directed to another unloading area. You will manually unload your metal into a large pile of metal objects. I always have to unload manually, as my truck has a contractor's rack over the bed. I unload my metal in about ten or fifteen minutes, it is not a big deal.

After you are unloaded, you head back to the front of the yard, re-weigh your empty truck on the same set of scales that you first weighed your load on, and then go back into the main office.

Hand the attendant your ticket. He or she will calculate the value all of your metals sold, and issue you a check for the full amount. It is as easy as that. The entire process should take you about half an hour, unless you have to wait in line to unload, which happens quite often.

I have been to a number of scrap yards, and the process is very similar at each one. If you have an additional trailer, you may have to go through the scales twice. The scrap yard may reverse the order of dropping of ferrous and non-ferrous metals. Other than that, things will go pretty much as I explained in this chapter.

PRECIOUS METALS: FAST, EASY MONEY

When most people think of selling scrap metal, they picture the loaded down pick-up trucks traveling down the highway with pieces of steel sticking out haphazardly from the overflowing bed. This is also where a lot of scrappers make their grocery money.

However, the real difference between the average scrapper and the successful businessperson is in their knowledge of the craft. Anybody can throw a bunch of junk into their trailer and make a couple of extra dollars, but the experienced scrapper knows that the real money in the scrap metal business is made in selling precious metals, such as gold, silver, and platinum.

Often, these precious metals, which can be valued at up to $1580 an ounce, can be found within larger pieces of machinery that is scrapped at the base scrap steel rate of near ten cents a pound!

Of course these precious metals are found in relatively meager amounts in these places, but it does not take much volume to net you a nice profit. The trick is to know where to locate the precious metals within the larger pieces of machinery. You have to do your research.

The easiest of the precious metals to find is copper (usually considered semi-precious). Almost all machinery and motors have copper inside them, due to copper's conductive properties. 95% of the wires that you find will have copper inside them.

Whenever you find copper, it is worth saving. Copper has a current spot price of $3.60 a pound. Even copper that is sealed inside motors and transformers can be sold at significantly increased rates over their base metals by selling it as copper breakage. Most scrap metal dealers will have a set rate for copper breakage, or electric motors, which currently sells for about thirty cents a pound, or three times more than scrap steel.

I remember the first time I took a load of scrap to the scrap metal yard. I had a truck bed overloaded with steel, and several large boxes of stripped copper. I was very surprised when the boxes of copper netted me almost as much money as the truck bed full of steel.

Again, copper is very easy to find. Start by saving all of the power cords that you see. If you see electrical items for free at garage sales, you should at least be saving the power cords for scrap copper. If something breaks or stops working in your home, cut the power cord off and save it. You should also disassemble appliances for interior copper and other precious metals.

The question often arises, as to whether the thrifty scrapper is further ahead to simply throw copper wires into a box and sell it as insulated copper, or to strip the insulation off and get the higher value for the non-insulated 'clean' copper. After doing a fair amount of research, the consensus seems to be that standard house wires and similar sized wires should be sold as insulated copper wires. Larger wires that would qualify as #1 copper should be stripped and sold as clean copper. Generally, #1 copper is considered to be any bare wire that is larger than a standard No.2 pencil lead and has a single layer of insulation. Anything smaller than that is #2 copper. #3 copper is telephone wires and computer cables.

Of course, if you have lots of spare time, feel free to make the extra profit and strip insulation to your heart's content, but remember - time is money.

Decorative solid copper items and copper tubing can also be found rather routinely at sales and thrift shops. Remember to keep your magnet with you. Non-magnetic clean copper can be sold for about $3 a pound. Non-magnetic copper coated ferrous metals are sold as copper breakage - thirty cents a pound.

You can also find gold and silver within the metal appliances and electronic scrap that you find discarded in various locations. This is where you can really make some extra dough. Silver currently spots at over $29 a troy ounce and gold sells for over $1580 a troy ounce. It does not take much gold or silver to make some nice money.

Where can I find this gold and silver, you may ask? Ah... That is question, isn't it? There is a ton of information on locating scrap silver and gold on the internet. Several excellent links have been provided for you in the free internet links at the end of this document.

To make a long story short, there are several locations where you can consistently find silver and gold in electronics and machinery. Computers have a fair amount of gold in the fingers on the connectors of the circuit boards, and also within the CPU processor chips. The older the computer is, the higher the gold content, in most cases. Some of the older circuit boards are actually gold plated.

Another good place to find silver and gold is in electrical contacts. While these contacts are often small and worth only 25 cents to a dollar, some silver contacts in vintage industrial machinery can be worth $20 a piece. I have found solid silver contacts in 1950s industrial lifts that weighed almost two ounces, or over $50 a piece!

This can be to your advantage, because a lot of the free electronics and machinery you are going to find are going to be old rusty vintage items. It is quite common to find 1950s or 60s electrical junk laying there in the woods, waiting for you to take it home and disassemble it.

Some other common places to find gold and silver is in thin interior wires in vintage electronics, some gold faced diodes in computers, vintage rotary telephone and telecommunications items, vintage video game systems, and inside cellular telephones.

I have provided an excellent link for several publications that I have bought and picked up a tremendous amount of information from, regarding the harvest of gold, silver and platinum from electronics, dental scrap, and other sources. I highly recommend that you check them out.

You can also find gold and silver quite regularly at sales and thrift shops, once you know what you are looking for. You would be surprised at how many sterling silver items that you can find at thrift shops once you get a knowledge base and start looking for them. Many of the people that price the items in thrift shops do not use current spot prices to price with, and you can often get a great bargain just by knowing the spot price and how to identify different types of precious metals.

There are many books and internet pages devoted to identifying gold and silver in its different forms, and also how to evaluate the gold content by using scratch-tests and strike sets. By all means, please take the time to research in this area while you are reading about how to find "Almost Free" items.

This book is devoted to locating free or almost free sources of income. You will not find "karat" gold or sterling silver items very often for cheap, but if you have done your homework, it is very possible to buy these items and resell them for a nice profit, so do your reading on this subject.

What we *are* going to discuss in this book is where to find gold and silver for free! Yes, that's right. I have found hundreds of dollars' worth of gold and silver just lying around in the woods and in junk piles, just waiting to be reclaimed. Does it have the romance of panning for gold in a mountain stream Out West? No, it doesn't. But the value is the same - gold is gold, plain and simple.

Where do we find this free gold and silver, you ask? Well, it's all around you. Gold and silver are among the most conductive of metals, which make them highly useful in a wide array of electronics and machinery. Gold and silver also are very resistant to abrasion and they do not oxidize (rust), which makes them the primary metals used in electronic contact points, and shiny surface coating for decorative items.

What is most important in locating gold and silver is to understand where it has been used. This is accomplished through diligent research, including the reading of this book. Remember, it does not take much gold or silver material to add up to significant profits.

If you can collect enough gold plated items or gold contacts to add up to one troy ounce of gold, then you have "mined" enough material to equal seven or eight large truck-loads of scrap steel! Gold currently spot-prices at close to $1620 a troy ounce. Silver, which is used more than gold, prices at close to $30 an ounce.

The historical price of gold is also important to understand (and silver historically parallels the gold price). The price of gold per ounce stayed fairly constant at between $35-40 from 1935 all the way up until 1971, when the US Dollar was removed from the Gold Standard. After 1971, the price of gold jumped from $40 an ounce to $150 an ounce by 1974, and then up to $615 by 1980. Do you think there's going to be a difference in how much gold was plated onto costume jewelry, gold rimmed plates, and eyeglass frames in 1968 when gold was $35 an ounce compared to 1995, when gold was $380 dollars an ounce? You betcha.

Even throughout the 1980s and 90s, gold stayed fairly steady at between $350 and $400, except for a spike in prices in the year 1980, when gold hit $615 an ounce. It wasn't until 2005 that the price of gold really skyrocketed. So, there is still significant gold to be found in items that are not all that old, relatively speaking.

That being said, the PRIME decade for finding the most gold and silver in electronics and decorations is from about 1961 to 1971. This is the time period when gold and silver had the most uses, and electronics from the era were often heavily plated with silver, and sometimes gold. Manufacturers were much more lenient in the application of gold and silver - remember, gold was only $35 an ounce, compared to over $1500 an ounce today.

It is common to find electronics from the 1960s for next to nothing at garage sales, thrift stores, or even laying in junk heaps. I guarantee you that there are thousands of these items in landfills near you right now. The electronics from the 60s are now over fifty years old – most items are broken, missing pieces, or downright outdated. A few are collector's items, but most are heavy, bulky clunkers that take up too much room in people's homes. Their loss is your gain.

Any time you see electronics for free, you should be grabbing and running. This is especially true, if they are from 1960-1985, or so. Not only do electronics from that era contain more gold than newer models, their interior components are also more valuable to sell on EBay, as we have discussed earlier.

WHERE TO FIND GOLD FOR CHEAP

We all know about the traditional methods of finding gold, including strip mining, gold panning, and dredging. All of them involve back-breaking labor and lots of money invested in order to get to the gold.

Why go through all this effort when there is gold to be found above ground for very little cost? We are going to talk about some specific items that you can find at garage sales, thrift stores, and in scrap piles for free.

First of all, look for scrap or discarded computers from the 1980s and 90s. You can find these computers for next to nothing. I have found quite a few computers in free boxes at sales and lying in the woods. They all have gold and silver inside, it is only a question of how much.

First, almost all motherboards contain gold in the connector fingers. Motherboards are the main circuit board inside the computer, and they will also have a heat sink with an IC chip underneath. The IC chip will also contain a significant amount of gold, and sometimes can be worth more than the spot gold value because of the collectible market of these chips to 'techies'. Check your EBay completed listings to see if the IC chip is worth more as a collectible piece.

Some of the older personal computers can have circuit boards that are completely lined with plated gold, and many of the connectors within the circuit boards also contain gold. Communications devices and high-tech items from the 1980s can also contain similar boards.

The circuit boards inside back planes and hard drives in computers also contain gold and silver in small amounts. These items are often more valuable sold as whole units than disassembled into smaller parts. The same is also true of RAM, or computer memory boards, which also contain small gold fingers. RAM is almost always more valuable when sold as whole boards than when the gold fingers are trimmed off of the boards. The smaller wires and the connector jacks that connect the wires to the circuit boards also often have gold or silver inside them.

Platinum can also be found in minute amounts in the platters of hard drives inside computers. These items can be saved and sold in large lots.

Gold can also be found inside of almost every cellular telephone. Some of the early cell phones can actually have a significant amount of gold in their circuitry, and these are the ones that you can find in junk piles and free boxes. All cell phones are worth money. If you see them, pick them up. If nothing else, there are many internet sites that offer a set price for scrap phones, dead or alive, so they are worth your time to pick them up.

Newer printer cartridges also contain gold in their contact buttons, which is why they also have a set scrap value on a number of internet sites.

There are many vintage items from the 60s and 70s that actually contain a fair amount of gold. Almost every item with a circuit board has gold or silver contacts. Some of the high- end electronics have large gold contacts. I once found a large factory loader from the 1960s that had interior gold contacts that added up to over ¼ ounce of pure gold, which is worth over $375 in today's gold market!

I have found that the 1960s audio equipment, including turntables, consoles, and radios will occasionally have silver coated copper wires throughout the entire main circuit board. These wires are always worth saving for precious metal refining. Almost all of these vintage audio items also have gold and silver contacts, and also have a fair amount of copper wiring inside.

Rotary telephones from the 1960s - early 1980s contain gold in their mouth pieces, and in several other internal contacts. The jacks of almost all telephones contain small amounts of gold inside the connectors.

There also many vintage items that you can find small amounts of gold in, where you would not expect to find gold. Such items would include: Some cologne and perfume caps, designer pens and pen holders, older trophies, dental work, lamps and lamp shades, gold colored trim in band uniforms and Rotary and Lions Club hats, Gold-trimmed china and dishes, picture frames, purse trim, lapel pins, clocks, cigarette holders, cuff-links, eyeglass frames, plaques, emblems, calculators, all switches, plug ends, telephone key pads, ribbon connectors, thermostatic contacts from high temperature items like popcorn poppers and electric skillets, coasters, waste baskets, vintage clothes gold-colored trim, coffee cups, and many more locations. If the item looks like it may possibly be gold, test it with your gold tester!

This subject is expanded on at one of our most popular pages titled Finding Gold and Silver on Garage Sale Academy.com.

1950s and 60s gold-colored lamps are fairly easy to find in thrift stores, as they are large by today's standards, and therefore sell slowly. Some of the these large lamps have a fair amount of gold plating in their bases, well worth the asking price at thrift stores, which is often $1-2.

There are many places that you can find items with interior components that you can sell, or scrap for metal value. You just have to use some ingenuity.

Besides finding items set out for free or discarded in the woods, you can also get these items for free by doing some leg-work. Think about where these items are going to show up.

Where do items that do not sell at garage sales go when the sales wrap up? In the garbage? Why not make yourself some business cards and give them to garage sales holders. Tell them you will haul away all their unsold items for free after the sale ends. You are going to get some junk, and may need access to a dumpster, but you will get a lot of good scrap metal and other items that we have discussed. For large sales, you may even get paid a nominal fee just to haul stuff away!

You can also make a classified ad or Craig's List ad that offers your services for removal of appliances, electronics and other items.

You could visit second-hand stores and antique shops and ask the manager if you could leave a large box for them to put broken or unsold vintage electronics, gold and silver plated items, etc. You may have a pay a small fee for each box-full of items, but probably not. Just start thinking about where dead electronics and appliances may be found, and you will come up more ideas on your own.

WHAT TO DO WITH YOUR GOLD AND SILVER CONTACTS

There are many investors looking to take advantage of the security of investing in gold and silver. The risk is considerably less than speculating on the stock market. Gold and silver are commodities with a finite supply. It is getting harder and harder to find, so the spot price is going to continue to trend upward over time.

The question for many gold and silver scrappers is: Do I save the scrap gold and silver and cash in several years after the gold prices advance, or do I cash in my gold immediately?

I have been saving my gold for several years now. I think that it's going to be a nice little kitty in several years, when our family is going to be paying for college tuitions. However, you may opt to cash in your gold, silver and platinum as you collect it. This can be accomplished in several ways.

First, you can send all of your contacts to an internet precious metals company, such as those listed in the Appendices in the back of the book. Keep in mind that if you sell your scrap gold to these companies, you will have to subtract your shipping costs in getting your gold to their location, and rely on their processes for evaluating the gold.

You can also take you contacts to a physical assayer or gold buyer in your area. They will assess the value of your gold or silver, and issue you a check for the value on site.

The third avenue for your consideration is more risky, but also will yield the highest value for your scrap precious metals. If you can effectively refine your own metal, you cut out several "middle-men", and get the most value from your hard work.

You must consider that the refining of precious metals is a risky business for beginners. The refining processes require the use of caustic materials, including acids. They also take some time and effort, and you will have to purchase chemicals and hardware to complete the refining.

If you choose to take this route, you do so at your own risk. Refining precious metals can emit noxious vapors and the acids can cause severe burns. You must have a secure area in which to refine, where you have ventilation system and can keep children away from. This is not a suggestion. It is necessity!

There are many different methods for refining precious metals, and I have not tried any of them, opting instead to hoard my gold and silver, with the eventual goal of selling to a reputable precious metal buyer. I do not recommend any one method of refinery. I t is up to you to decide after completing your research.

There are many different methods for refining precious metals, which can be found online through your research. Websites for refining gold and silver from electronic scrap can be found in the Links at the end of the document.

NOTES ON PRECIOUS METALS IN COINS!

Quickly answer the following question: How much is a U.S. Quarter Dollar worth? Twenty-five cents, you say? Not so fast, my friend.

The average person walking down the street will tell you that a quarter is a quarter. They are all worth twenty-five cents. That is true, if you are spending the quarter in a store. But, if you are a knowledgeable investor, you know that the quarter is currently worth $5.23 if it is from 1963 or before, due to the metal composition of the coin.

All quarters minted before 1964 contain 90% silver. The same is true of dimes from the same period. Even war nickels minted from 1942-45 contain 35% silver, and are worth $1.35 at today's melt value. For a complete list of melt values for circulated coins, check the Links at the end of this document.

90% silver coins are tough to find on the street. Consider yourself very lucky if you receive a silver coin as change in a payment transaction. There are not many of these left in circulation, due to people knowing the value of the silver contained in the coins. That being said, there is nothing wrong with checking your piggy bank to see if there is some silver in there!

The melt value also gives you a reference point, so that you can determine if you want to buy silver coins if you find them at flea markets, antique stores, or garage sales (rarely). Many antique store owners do not frequently update their prices, and the silver spot price can shoot up from time to time, allowing you to pick up silver below the spot price.

Even if the silver is priced at spot, you may elect to buy the coins, and save them to sell when the spot price rises. Silver and gold are very dependable investment options; much safer than stocks. There is only so much metal that is left to be mined or reclaimed. The price is going to go up eventually. It's only a matter of when, and how much.

Silver coins can be hard to find at an affordable price, but one coin that you can easily find that has a definitive spot price is copper pennies. I remember researching scrap metals on EBay, and seeing people buying bag fulls of pennies. I was intrigued. Why are people buying pennies when they are only worth one cent?

Then, I thought about it a little more. It's all about volume and investment. All U.S. pennies minted before 1986, and Canadian pennies minted before 1994 are made of 95% copper. A 1980 Lincoln penny is currently worth almost three cents in melt value, although it is illegal to melt the coins down for copper (it is NOT illegal to melt down old silver coins, for some reason). Regardless, the coins still contain a specified amount of copper, and are traded based on that value. The value of copper is also on the rise. Start saving your old pennies. Ten years from now you will be glad that you did.

NOTES ON SATELLITE DISHES AND RECEIVERS

A person could make a nice side-job business by offering to remove unsightly decaying satellite dishes from people's yards for a nominal fee, or for free, if that does not work. You can also stop at homes that have these old dishes, and offer your service in removing them. Many people will be appreciative to you for cleaning up their yards or homes.

Start looking for these old outdated, non-functioning satellite dishes and you will see them everywhere. Look for the huge 3-4' wide mesh dishes from the 1980s and early 90s. None of the systems that these dishes were designed for are in use anymore. Also look for the older model DIRECTV and Dish Network dishes. They will usually be sun faded and have green mildew or moisture marks on them.

Many of them are even on ground level, so you don't have to mess with climbing ladders and getting on roofs. People don't have any use for them anymore, but they do not want to take the time or make the effort to remove them.

This is great for you. You can remove dishes on ground level in about fifteen minutes. All you have to do is cut the pole off and throw the whole pole and dish into your truck and you are done. Disassemble the dish from the pole later at your facility.

Cut the sod or turf in a circle around the hole and attempt to save the grass for when you are done. Dig down about 8" around the base of the pole. Make the hole wide enough to get a reciprocating or cut-off saw (or a hacksaw, if you don't have access to a cut-off saw) into. Cut the pole off level with the ground. Trim any cords that are showing. Put a small board over the stump of the pole, so it does accidentally cut someone's feet if it gets dug up. Cover the board with dirt level with the yard. Replace the sod, if you were successful in saving it. If not, you may elect to carry a small bag of grass seed with you to fix the hole that you made.

You should also ask the resident there is they have the receiver box or remote control for the dish that you removed for them. The receivers contain large circuit boards that you can harvest precious metals from. The remote controls also have small boards inside.

Why go through the hassle of removing dishes? Gold. There is gold and silver in all satellite transponders, and there is quite a bit in the older large dishes, and even the first generation DirecTV dishes. The transponder is the plastic piece in the center of the dish that receives the signal from the satellite itself. The dish itself is also usually magnetic stainless and if you have a good number of these, you can get a higher rate for the stainless than normal shred value for steel.

But, back to the gold. I just opened up several transponders from vintage dishes to see what was inside them. I was surprised to find that the entire circuit boards inside several transponders were plated in gold, and there were several other interior components that had gold in them too. The circuitry also was lined with silver. The jacks were brass, with gold pins.

To get at the interior circuit boards, hit the seam on the transponder with a hammer to split it open. The circuit board comes out very easily.

SELLING SCRAP METAL ON EBAY

It is easy and profitable to sell scrap metal on eBay. I have found that I consistently make more cash per pound, selling solid copper and brass on eBay than I do selling the same materials at a scrap yard.

I will go through this process, as I did for selling metal at a scrap yard.

First, go onto the USPS website and order yourself a selection of Priority Mail shipping boxes. All of these boxes are free to order, and have no shipping charges. The USPS wants customers shipping items by Priority Mail, as it makes them more money than the same items shipped Parcel Post or First Class Mail.

Get a variety of sizes of boxes, but make sure that you get the large regular Priority Mail and Large Flat Rate Priority Mail boxes, plus some smaller regular Priority Mail and Medium Flat Rate boxes.

Once you get the boxes, start collecting your scrap metal in the Large Flat Rate Boxes, especially solid metal copper and brass. The copper box will probably contain copper pipes, ornamental copper items, and copper connectors, etc. The brass box could have ornamental brass objects, plumbing fixtures, etc. Many scrap metal dealers require you to keep brass bullet casings separate from other brass, as there are small amounts of other metals in casing primers.

Once you fill up a Flat Rate box with one type of scrap, you are ready to sell it on eBay. Weigh your box with the metal contents inside it on a scale with a digital read-out.

Take a digital photo of the scale, with the weight of the box displayed on the readout of your scale, so that your potential bidders on eBay can be confident in the accuracy of your auction. These potential bidders will be bidding based almost entirely on the weight of the scrap metal in the box, so they will want to be able to verify the exact weight of the product.

Next, dump out the box on a flat surface and take some photographs of the contents. If you have ornamental items in your box, take additional photos of those items.

Next, download the photos to your computer, and then log in to your eBay account. Go to the 'Sell an Item' page on eBay. There are two categories that you can sell scrap metal in: Coins and Paper Money, Bullion and Business & Industrial, Metals & Alloys. List your scrap metal in one of these two categories.

Go to the photograph section and upload your digital photographs to your auction listing page.

An example of a title that I would use for my auction would be along the lines of: '24# (LBS)

#1 SCRAP COPPER Bowls Pipes Decorations'. #1 Copper is the designation scrap dealers use for solid copper items, or large stripped copper wires with no insulation, and is the highest grade of copper. The additional descriptors may also get collectors of ornamental copper items to bid on your auction.

Make sure that you are accurate in your description of the auction. Subtract the weight of the box when providing the weight (usually about 8 ounces for a Large Flat Rate box). Under the Shipping section of the listing, click on 'Large Flat Rate Box', and use the 'Calculated Shipping' option, with an additional $1-2 added, so that some of your eBay and PayPal fees are covered by the shipping cost.

List your auction. I like to start my auctions between 3:00 and 9:00 PM, as that as when the most users are on eBay.

When the auction is complete, seal the Flat Rate Box, address it with the winning bidder's address, and take it to the post office to ship it, or if you are already an internet seller, use your online shipping service and ship from home. It is as easy as that!

TO KEEP ASSEMBLED, OR DISASSEMBLE; THAT IS THE QUESTION!

One of the more difficult decisions in maximizing profits on large pieces of vintage electronics or machinery is figuring out whether to sell the entire item on EBay, or to take the item apart and sell the interior components.

There are several things that will affect your decision. The first is the overall size of the item. It is common to find large appliances, console stereos, exercise equipment and other similar-sized items with a 'FREE' sign on them along the roadways in any small town. Should you pick them up? Heck yes, you should.

The question then becomes, how do I sell this bulky piece of junk? Obviously, nobody is going to pay the shipping fees for shipping these items weighing several hundred pounds, unless the item is extremely valuable.

It is possible that you can sell the item on EBay, with a free local pickup option for the shipping method. The winning bidder then has to make arrangements with you to pick up the item after the auction is completed.

You can also list the item on Craigslist or in the local classified section of your newspaper. Selling the item whole is often the fastest and least time-intensive method of selling large items. There is almost zero preparation time, and you can often unload items in one week or less.

You should sell items whole if you determine that the item is collectible in the condition you find it in (no restoration costs to you), and if you think somebody near you would want to buy it. This is often the case with audio equipment, juke boxes, large advertising items, and arcade games. These types of items have many collectors, and they will buy whole items whether they work or not.

There are some issues to consider when selling whole items, such as the ones that we have discussed. The most important issue is that in order for you to sell the item, you have to know whether it works, or not. If you advertise that the item works, it had better be completely functional. This is especially true if you sell your item on EBay, as you do not want to receive negative feedback from your buyers, or nobody will want to bid on your auctions.

You may decide to advertise the item in 'As-Is' condition, which means that buyer or bidder is buying your item as they see it in the ad or auction page. 'As-Is' condition means that you are unsure of the operating condition of the machinery and components, or that you know that the machine does not work. This is often a safer way of selling large pieces of machinery with many moving parts.

You also have to keep in mind that old machinery that has not been used for a long period of time will often break down quickly when it is put back into use. In other words, if you test something for a couple of minutes and it seems to work fine, it may still break very soon after your buyer starts using the item. Then, you have to deal with possibility of having the buyer leave you negative feedback or having to at least partially refund the sales price because the item broke. Imagine how you would feel if you bought a cool collectible vintage juke box, and then it broke down after you played less than ten songs on it. You'd want your money back, right?

I honestly have sold very few large whole items, due to the problems I've already discussed. Nobody wants to pay shipping costs on these types of items, and gas prices prevent people from driving long distances to pick them up.

It is also routinely more profitable to disassemble large items and sell the components on eBay. I can remember multiple occasions, where I attempted to sell electronic items that weighed between ten and seventy pounds on eBay and received no bids at under $10, due to the shipping costs. After I received no bids, I disassembled the electronics and sold the components for 5 to 10 times that amount within several weeks.

One good example of this was a vintage 1960s console stereo / record player that we found at a garage sale for $5. We hauled it home and put in our basement. It worked great! It had a sharp looking wooden cabinet, and contained a radio, a record turntable, and even an 8- track player with some old working Elvis, Aerosmith and Johnny Cash tapes. I don't remember the manufacturer, but it was a mid-range brand name that I was familiar with. In other words, it was not a top-of-the-line collectible brand.

Everything worked great on the console, and I used it a lot when we first got it, and then less and less frequently over time. Eventually, we decided that the console took up a lot of room, and we wanted to go another route with décor in the basement, so we tried to sell the stereo.

We listed the whole console on eBay for $20, with a free local pickup shipping method. It did not receive a bid for three re-lists at $20.

My wife wanted to put the console out for free at the roadside, but I said no. Even though this was at the beginning of our selling careers, I knew enough to take apart the console and try to sell the interior parts.

It has been about seven years since we sold the console, but from my recollection, it took about four hours to completely take it apart. It took a couple of hours to research which parts to sell on EBay, and another couple of hours to list the items. After about two weeks, I had sold the 8- track tapes for $20, the 8-track player for about $25, some parts off of the turntable for $15, two sets of large interior speakers for $35, the cloth wiring for $10, the tuner assembly for $15, and then scrapped the rest for another $20-30 in scrap copper and other metals. If I knew then what I know now, I would have made another $20-30 in selling name plates, the turntable stylus, the cloth speaker coverings, and other items, and also an extra $10+ in scrap gold and silver contacts. You get the point.

Recently, I helped my mother remove a 10-year old treadmill exercise machine from her house. I took it apart in less than an hour, and sold the motor for $25, the digital display for $15, the rollers for $10, the track for $5, and it had about $25 worth of scrap metal in it afterwards.

I found a dead Pioneer tuner stereo at a garage sale for free about three years ago, and sold the oak case for $50, the metal screw-on feet for almost $20, and the name plate for another $10. I sold assorted components for another $20, and there was about $10 worth of scrap metal inside, mostly copper, aluminum and brass. These are not just isolated incidents, I find this stuff all of the time.

If you think about it, the selling of components makes much more sense on many levels. The shipping cost for these smaller components is usually going to be under $10. People can afford to pay for shipping for parts, rather than paying significantly higher shipping costs for whole units.

There are many, many collectors of these types of vintage electronics. If you can think of a popular type of electronics, somebody probably collects them. Collectors enjoy tinkering with interior components, upgrading parts, and customizing their units. Plus, old systems often break down and parts fail. In other words, people that like these old machines need parts often, and they are the type of people who enjoy being on a computer and buying things online.

Vintage components are also very difficult to find at physical stores, even in metropolitan areas. Do remember seeing stores that sell vintage audio or computer components? Me either. It's much easier to go to eBay and find what you are looking for there, than to locate a physical store that sells vintage replacement parts.

MAXIMIZE PROFITS IN VINTAGE ELECTRONICS

There are several things that you will want to research BEFORE you take apart any vintage electronic item.

As we discussed before, research Completed Items on EBay, and determine which components are worth selling. Again, you should know ahead of time which assemblies are better sold whole, and which assemblies should be broken down into even smaller components, or individual parts.

I have also provided you with an excellent free resource in the Links which describes in detail how to disassemble many different large electronics and appliances for scrap value.

Once you have an idea of which parts you will be removing for sale, take your item to a location where you can make a mess, but not lose any small parts. A large table top or countertop works well.

Gather your tools. The tools you will use most often are: both types of screwdrivers, needle-nose pliers, wire cutters, an adjustable wrench, a hammer (Oh, yeah! Breaking' stuff is fun!), a magnet, several large vinyl trash bag, and safety glasses and gloves.

You can expedite the process with a cordless drill or power screwdriver with both driver bits. A power rotary tool (Dremel) with a supply of cut-off disks and a drill bit is well worth the investment, if you do not have one. I use mine constantly.

You may also need a set of sockets, and you will occasionally find exotic screw heads like star bits and Allen wrench heads, but if you have a Dremel, you can cut off the screws, or make them into standard screwdriver heads by slicing them with the cut-off disk. You will also use the Dremel often for cutting off rusted or stripped screws and bolts. It also cuts through thick copper cord insulation like butter, saving you tons of time!

Please heed a word of caution. Before you start breaking stuff, make sure you know what you are doing. Remember, in the 1950s and 60s, nobody even knew what a 'health code violation' was. Old electronics and appliances can contain some nasty stuff. There is mercury inside some old glass switches and components, for instance. You should not open anything that is sealed in glass, or welded shut, unless you know for sure what is inside.

OK, now that we got that out of the way, let's break some stuff. Start on the outside and CAREFULLY remove any decorative items, advertising badges, knobs, feet, etc., that you can sell. Remember, the plastic is going to be old and brittle on vintage items. If you snap the emblem in half, it is worthless. Believe me, I have broken some, even though I was being very careful. Even the glass in the display covers is more brittle in many older components.

After the outer pieces are removed, check eBay Completed Listings to see if the outer shell of your item can be sold. Often, the shells and cases of audio components, and even rotary telephones can be sold.

I usually start by using the cordless drill and unscrewing all of the screws that I can see on the outside of the device. Remove the outer shell, or the access panel to get at the interior of the item. If the shell is going to be sold, put it in your 'Sell' pile. If it is not going to be sold and it is plastic, throw it in your trash bag. If it is metal, hit it with a magnet. If it is ferrous, throw it in your 'Steel' pile. Sometimes the shell will be aluminum and should be saved in its own pile with other aluminum.

I save all of my screws, bolts and other connectors, as well. I put them all in a large coffee can. When it's full, I intend to sell the lot on eBay in the vintage electronics category for about $20. I also sometimes use various screws when I need them for household repairs, or sometimes screws are sold with components, and I need to replace a couple that I lost. Occasionally, you will find screws and bolts made of solid brass or aluminum. Save these in their respective scrap pile.

Now that you are into the interior of the item, find the components that you are looking to sell, and remove them. Put them in your Sell pile. Save the screws and attachments that affix the items that you are going to sell if possible and sell them with the component. If you lose a screw, do not worry about it. The screws are just for insurance, in case the buyer needs them. They are not required.

Try to avoid clipping wires connected to components that you plan to sell. Carefully pull wires that have jacks or plugs from their ports using needle-nose pliers. Remember, your buyer is going to be hooking the component into his system, and is not going to want to splice wires, if it is avoidable.

If there are multiple components available to buy on eBay, and some of the listings have the entire wires, with the plugs, and yours have clipped ends, your item will not get many bids, or will not sell if it is a fixed price auction.

Once all of your sellable components have been removed, the fun starts. Take one last look, and see if there might be anything else that you could sell that you did not find on eBay before. When you are satisfied that everything that could be sold has been removed, you are ready to start scrapping.

You should realize that there are also whole components that can be sold as scrap, on eBay, via an E-Scrap website, or at your local scrap yard. Internet sites such as Boardsort.com offer fixed prices for items such as computer hard drives, circuit boards, cellular telephones, and computer power supply boxes. You should check these sites so that you know what you will be saving, and the prices that are offered. Several of these sites are listed in the appendices of this document, with hyperlinks to their websites.

Now that you know what you are looking for, get out your USPS Priority Mail Flat Rate Boxes. Label the boxes with the materials that you intend to place in them. In addition, you will need extra-large boxes or totes for ferrous steel, and medium and low class circuit boards. You will have a lot of these materials.

I normally collect a fair amount of vintage electronics and appliance parts before I have a disassembly session, so that I can get a lot of scrap to sell at one time.

When I start scrapping, I always have the following Large Flat Rate boxes ready for material collection: Bare Copper, Insulated Copper, Bare Brass (It is OK to have copper attached to brass, and most scrap yards allow chrome covering over brass, as well), old aluminum, shiny aluminum (often aluminum heat sinks), and a smaller box for silver and gold contacts and components I intend to break down for precious metal content.

If there are computer hard drives in the pile, they usually require their own special boxes for material that will be sold separately, or sent to Boardsort.

I usually keep another box of copper / aluminum heat sinks, and later take the Dremel to the copper wire. If you use the cut-off disk on the Dremel, you can slice the copper all the way down to the spool, and then peel off the copper. Place the copper in your shiny copper box, and save the heat sink bases. They are often stainless steel, and can be sold separately at scrap yards for decent money. You will find a lot of large heat sinks in old electronics and appliances. I found a heat sink several days ago in a 1950s industrial washing machine that had ten pounds of copper spooled inside it. The stainless base weighed 18 pounds.

I also save all of my plug ends from electrical cords in a box, and later peel the prongs off with pliers or cut open the plug end with the Dremel, and remove the metal. Older plug have brass prongs, and most newer plugs are made of shiny aluminum. You are required to cut the plug ends off of copper electrical cords before you can sell them at the scrap dealer, so you will be cutting off the plug ends, anyway.

Boardsort also offers a fixed rate for wire and cord connectors that contain gold. Many computer connectors that resemble bristles at the ends, or have many tiny holes contain small amounts of gold and silver. Ribbon ends also frequently contain precious metals. You may decide to save these connectors in a box, and sell them on eBay, as well.

Most scrap dealers also buy components containing copper as 'Copper Breakage' or 'Electric Motors'. Save components containing copper in a box. Many of these components can also be easily broken open with a hammer or cut open with a Dremel, and then you can remove the copper and brass pieces that are inside to maximize your profits.

Make sure that you are keeping an eye out for precious metal contacts while you are scrapping. Old electronics and appliances can have relatively large contacts that are often pure silver, and sometimes gold. Look on the ends of brass and copper fingers where wires are connected, inside all electric motors, and inside any components that spin at high speeds or generate a lot of heat.

Contacts can range in size from the width of a pencil lead all the way up to the diameter of a large watch battery. Many gold contacts will be bright and shiny gold-colored buttons. They are easy to spot, as gold does not tarnish. Silver contacts can be more difficult to find, as they are often dulled and tarnished with age, and can blend in with the base material.

If you are unsure if the contacts are silver or gold, lightly scrape them with a screwdriver, or hit them with the Dremel disk. The will be bright and shiny under the exterior coating of grime. If you're still not sure, test with your gold tester, or throw them in your 'Gold and Silver' box and refine it with the rest of the material in the box later.

When you find good contacts, clip the button of silver or gold off, and then keep the base material for brass or copper scrap. Don't waste the whole brass or copper finger by refining it in your gold and silver material.

When you fill up the Flat Rate boxes, photograph the materials inside, weigh the box (take a photo of the box with the scale read-out), label the box with the weight, and then list the material on eBay, or save it to take to the scrap dealer.

The last step is the most important. Make sure that you clean up your mess after you are done bashing electronics! If you do your business inside, your significant other will not be happy with the end result of your destruction. If they are not happy, then you will not be happy either, right?

If you have an outdoor shop or disassembly area, you should still clean up the mess. Metal pieces can be sharp, and kids or pets can get cut on them.

TREATING YOUR BUSINESS AS A BUSINESS: INCOME TAX ISSUES

You don't have to be an accountant or a business major in college to effectively manage your small business. In my opinion, the one thing that keeps the majority of internet sellers from graduating from a small-time operation into a real business is the failure to understand where they are making money and where they are losing profits.

On the surface this sounds like it would be common sense, but often, the sources of the issues are not as evident as you would think. Anybody can look at their checking accounts and see how much money eBay or Amazon is depositing into them. But is that the bottom line profits of your business? Of course not.

I highly recommend keeping track of your profits and expenses on a spreadsheet, so that you can get a picture of your overall money flow.

There are many different spreadsheets online that you can tailor to your selling situation. Find one that you like and start using it from the outset of your selling or scrapping career. You will be very glad that you did.

Keeping your spreadsheet helps you in a number of different ways. First, you can see which segments of your selling are making you the most money. Second, you can find areas where you can save yourself money in over-expenditure on packaging supplies, storage fees, gas money, etc.

To illustrate the second point, I remember reviewing our numbers after one season of garage sailing. We thought that we were doing really well, because we were making good profits on a very high percentage of the items that we bought. However, after crunching numbers, we were not as happy. We were losing a lot of our profits in gas costs and meals while driving from sale to sale. Also, a lot of the items were we selling were large, bulky items, and were costing us more money for packaging supplies. We also realized that we were spending a lot of time and money driving to the post office with packages.

These discoveries that we made directly led to us changing where we bought inventory, how we kept track of travel expenses, and investing in using an internet postage and pick-up service.

Keeping track of your expenses also prepares you for completing your income taxes. Not only are you required to claim your income from internet sales on your income tax returns, your internet sales business can actually help you with your tax burden, or increase your refund.

This is especially true in the first year of your business, as you are allowed to claim start-up expenses for expenditures, such as computers, smart phones, Wi-Fi and high speed internet installation, storage units, shelving, desks and furniture, and other odds and ends that you need to start your business. Just ensure that you are using the items that you are going to claim as business expenses only for your business. If you use any of the items for personal use in any manner, you will need to adjust for this personal use. Failure to do so, could lead to large fines if you are audited.

Keeping you receipts organized is also very important. Not only does that allow you to see where you are spending your money, it is also necessary to be able to verify spending to claim them on your income tax returns. You can claim meals and other expenses while you are conducting your business (finding inventory), overhead costs (packaging tape, computer paper, etc.), and advertising expenses, but only if you have receipts to verify your claims.

Another very nice tax deduction you can claim is for your home office. If you have a portion of your home or other building that is used EXCLUSIVELY for the execution of your business, you can claim that portion of your home's utilities, repairs, and property taxes on your income taxes. That can be a huge break. You can also claim the cost of the degradation to your office space and the furniture and appliances that you use in your business. All of the forms needed to claim these items are found on tax preparation applications, such as TurboTax. You may have to do some research, or ask you tax professional, but the time will be well spent.

Just make sure that you understand that if you claim a home business deduction, you will be more likely to be audited at some point. Ensure that you have reviewed the applicable IRS rules, and have receipts and paperwork to verify your deductions.

DONATIONS

Another way that you can save money is to donate items to Goodwill or similar non- profit organizations. This would include both your own personal items and your business inventory items that did not sell at auction or on Amazon.

One website that will greatly assist you in this area is www.ItsDeductible.com. The website provides you an acceptable allowance to claim for a wide array of household items in two condition categories. For instance, a used vinyl record in average condition may be claimed for $2. The values are accepted by the IRS. You may be surprised how much a large box of clothing will allow you claim on you taxes. You can also claim the mileage for you to get from your home to the donation site.

You do not get to claim 100% of the value of the donations to Goodwill, but the amount that you can claim can be significant, if you donate continually throughout the year.

Make sure that you take pictures of the contents of the boxes and bags that you donate, and save them in a folder on your computer, so that you can verify what you have donated.

ItsDeductible is also partnered with TurboTax, and other tax prep applications. This allows the tax applications to directly download your information from your donations and mileage on your ItsDeductible page, and place the values in the correct areas of your return.

This is a huge time saver!

THANK YOU, READERS!

Thank you for taking the time to read this book. I hope that you enjoyed it as much as I enjoyed researching the background content and putting this book together.

Please put your mind to immediately applying what you learned here in Almost Free Money. DO NOT wait until next week or next month to start! You can find items to sell in any location, and at any time of the year.

YOU have to make up your mind to get the ball rolling, and it will be all downhill from there. I hope that you will have as much fun as my family and I have finding treasure for free, or plucking dusty gems from garage sales and thrift stores.

If you have any questions, contact me on my Facebook page, at Garage Sale Academy's Forum, on Twitter, or email me at almostfreemoney@yahoo.com. I would like to hear from you! Reminder: The Almost Free Money Nation newsletter provides lots of great freebies and is a very helpful source of information for used item flippers and garage sale shoppers. It is free to join and you can even use your Facebook account to sign up.

If you feel that this book has helped you to find new and enjoyable ways to make money or save your family cash, I humbly ask you for only two things. #1, tell your family and friends about this book, and #2, please take several seconds to leave a 5-star review regarding this book on its Amazon Detail Page at http://www.amazon.com/dp/B00HUCT90S. Positive feedback directly affects other readers' reviews and leads to additional orders, and the proceeds from this book will go directly into my sons' college funds.

Thanks again, and please proceed to the Appendices, where over 500 specific items that you can find are listed, and also over 20 links are provided to aid in further research and enhancement of the knowledge that was provided in Almost Free Money.

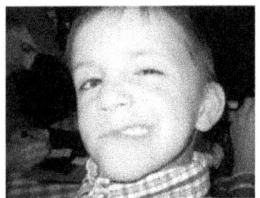

WEBSITES AND LINKS

Here are some very helpful websites and web pages to jump start your research. These are my favorites, after many hours of surfing (You are welcome!)

1. http://www.scrapmetaljunkie.com/scrap-metal-handbook-guide

I still can't believe this site is free. A tremendous amount of information, and well organized. The site provides a nice explanation on how to sort and identify scrap metals.

This is the only site that I have found that provides step-by-step instructions on how to disassemble appliances and other large items for maximizing scrap recovery.

Includes: How to take apart a TV, Computer, Washing Machine, Microwave, and many more items. Also has an excellent blog, with information from many experienced scrappers. Regardless of whether you are a beginner, or an experienced scrapper, if you have not been to this site, you will make money by spending time here.

2. http://www.scribd.com/doc/20327561/Scrap-Parts-Comp-Identification#outer_page_1

Scraper's Master Parts List: A nice summation of where you can find valuable gold, silver and platinum in computers and other electronics.

Indexed, with photo identification of components like diodes, transformers, and capacitors and where to find them within the electronics.

3. http://boardsort.com

This company will pay you up front through PayPal immediately upon confirmation of your information with digital photo of your material. They pay competitive prices for computer scrap, gold board fingers, and some other related e-scrap. You have to pay for shipping, but they pay up front, which is nice. They also have an updated price list of what they pay for a variety of materials, so you know what you can expect to be paid when you send them your scrap.

4. http://voices.yahoo.com/find-almost-free-gold-thrift-shops-yard-sales-beginner-113530.html?cat=51

Also has a link for finding silver. Good explanation of the different classifications of gold and silver, their markings on jewelry, and how to find it for cheap at garage sale, thrift shops, etc.

5. http://fairsalvage.com/material_info.html

A sample page from a scrap metal yard - good descriptions of different classifications of scrap.

6. http://fairsalvage.com/pricing_clare.html

A sample price list from the same scrap yard.

7. http://www.ehow.com/how_7830442_refine-gold-plating.html

How to refine your scrap and plated gold to .995 pure. Requires chemicals and safety equipment. Do this at your own risk.

8. http://shorinternational.com/RefineAgInstruct.php

How to refine plated silver and silver contacts to .995 pure silver. Alternate method using household chemicals. Do this at your own risk.

9. http://cointrackers.com/is-my-coin-silver.php

Good information on silver coins, and actual silver content. Did you know that a 1963 USquarter is worth $2.09 due to silver content?!

10. https://www.auctiva.com

eBay listing web site. We use this exclusively for making our EBay listings. You get free templates and scrolling display, which lets visitors on your auctions see all of your other ongoing auctions. Auctiva also allows you to use an unlimited number of photos in your listings. Creates professional-looking auctions, which helps breed confidence with bidders. Current price $15.99 a month, after free trial for new users.

11. https://itsdeductibleonline.intuit.com

As discussed in Donations section. Provides IRS-accepted values for your donations, and keeps track of your donations for the entire tax year. Inserts your donations into online Income tax forms such as TurboTax.

12. http://used.addall.com

Free book search with values, used for finding values for rare and collectible books. Save this to your favorites, you should be using this site on a regular basis.

13. http://pulse.ebay.com

Provides a 'Hot List' for EBay completed listings. There is a drop-down box at the top for searching specific categories.

14. http://www.isoldwhat.com

Has entire listing of EBay categories, and also number of individual listings for each category and subcategory. Also has Amazon browse counts by category.

15. http://www.metalprices.com

Spot prices for most precious and scrap metals, plus historical prices, with graphs.

RECOMMENDED PAY SITES:

1. Buy Low on EBay, Sell High on Amazon

An excellent and affordable program that teaches you how a top-rated Amazon seller made over $100,000 buying items on EBay and re-selling quickly on Amazon. Well-organized information - anybody can make money on this document!

2. The Complete Battery Reconditioning Report

This document pays for itself, as soon as you recondition your first battery instead of buying a new one. I use this information all the time. Very easy to use information on how to recharge supposedly dead NiCad, NiMH and Lead Acid batteries. Most of the techniques can be applied for free, and the author gives you an excellent and unique way to start a new or second income in any locale. Highly recommended.

3. How to Make Money in the Home-Based Salvage and Recycling Business

The Author does an excellent job giving step by step instructions for starting your own business or second income by recycling scrap metal and electronics. Personal stories about how the author got started and took his business to the next level.

He provides many examples of materials that you can make good money on that you can find anywhere. Includes salvage of gold and silver from electronics. Well-organized and easy to read. Also affordable, as well. Worth the cost of the document.

4. Worm Farming: A Green Way to Earn Easy Money

How to start a nice side business selling worms for multiple uses, including fishing bait. You also produce excellent mulch for your own garden, and can sell the mulch / fertilizer for use in others' gardens. A neat "green" idea for making money with very little effort and almost no start-up costs. Affordable price, currently $17.

5. 250 Ways to Make Money

Many ways to make money in your spare time, most without any start-up costs. This e-book is very affordable at under $10, and has many real-world ideas for making money, to add to your knowledge base.

6. How to Make Money Buying and Selling Gold

Everything you need to start a business or second income buying gold items, including scrap gold.

7. Make Money Flipping Craig's List and EBay Items

Guaranteed system for finding items, primarily on Craigslist reselling for quick profits, either on EBay or re-listing items for higher prices on Craigslist.

Includes a Top 10 list of the best-selling items, and a proven step by step process for starting this venture. Really quick and easy, this system also comes with a 60 day money back guarantee, in case you are too lazy to take advantage of all this great information. This is an underutilized source for quick money in many locales, and the author has perfected the process over several years making a lot of money with very little cost.

REMINDER: The category number in the Appendices tables refers to the eBay category number that you should list that particular item in. Just cut-and-paste the number into the eBay category number box on the eBay listing page, or into the Category Search Bar.

- If you are viewing in large font sizes, it may distort the edges of the tables. You may wish to order the Softcover or DVD version of Almost Free Money. The table is optimized for Kindle Fire, but it is impossible to size this table for all readers, due to Kindle format limitations.

SMD – Scrap Metal Dealer   VI – Various Internet Sites   E – E-Scrap Sites, like Boardsort   EM – eBay Motors

APPENDIX 1: DEFINED VALUE ITEMS

#	ITEM	CAT.	DESCRIPTION
1	Air Conditioner Compressors	SMD	$3
2	Alternators, Vehicle	SMD	Abt $4
3	Auto Bodies	SMD	$300+
4	Batteries, Lithium-Ion	SMD	At least .60/LB
5	Calculators, Graphing	VI	$4-20
6	Cam Corders	VI	
7	Cameras, Digital	VI	
8	Cartridges, Ink Toner	VI	
9	Catalytic Converters	VI, SMD	

10	Cellular Telephones	VI	Working Phones to $80, Junk phones still $4
11	Circuit Boards Gold Fingers	E	
12	Circuit Boards, Clean	E	
13	Circuit Boards, Populated E-Scrap Sites High	E	Gold Fingers, Content, Low -VCRs, TVs, etc
14	Computer Backplanes	E	
15	Computer Daughter Boards	E	
16	Computer Diodes	E	
17	Computer EPROMS	E	
18	Computer Hard Drive Boards	E	
19	Computer Hard Drives -Whole	E	
20	Computer IC Chips	E	
21	Computer Memory	E	
22	Computer Mother Boards	E	
23	Computer Processors -PCUs	E	Ceramic, older CPUS can be collectible -Big $
24	Oxygen Sensors, Vehicle	VI	Abt $3 / LB

25	Pager Boards	E	
26	Printer Cartridges, Empty	VI	Values $1.25 - $20
27	Radiators, AL	SMD	$3
28	Radiators, Copper	SMD	$15, or $1.65 /LB
29	SIM, Smart Card Scrap	E	
30	Starters, Vehicle	SMD	Abt $4
31	Tantalum Resistors, Chips		TantalumRecyclers.com
32	Telecom Boards	E	
33	Text Books	VI	Usually better on Amazon
34	Transistors	E	
35	Transmissions, Vehicle	SMD	$10-35
36	Video Game Systems	VI	
37	Wheels, Aluminum	SMD	$10 each

APPENDIX 2: EBAY COLLECTIBLE

#	ITEM	CAT.	DESCRIPTION
1	1950s Items	69853	
2	1960s	69854	Items Retro, Hippie items Lucite, Bakelite
3	1970s Items	69855	
4	Advertising Items	34	Colas, John Deere, Recognizable Logos. Pick Up any Free Items w/Advertising
5	Aprons	13951	
6	Archery, Vintage Items	158960	Broad heads, Wood Arrows, Ads, Bows
7	Ash Trays	594	
8	Autographs and Signed Items	14429	
9	Automobilia, Collectibles	14024	License Plates, Spark Plugs, Advertising
10	Aviation items	14049	
11	Bakelite Plastic Items	72397	If you don't know what Bakelite is, find out!
12	Banks	66503	
13	Beads, Vintage	156281	Bakelite, Retro, Ceramics best

14	Bears, Teddy	386	
15	Beer Collectibles	562	Advertising, Signs, Tins, Cans, Bottle Caps
16	Bikes, Vintage	159000	Frames Parts Frames, Handle Bars, Forks, Guards, Pedals
17	Billiards Balls	75192	
18	Boat and Ship items	14052	
19	Bottle Caps	158421	Look for Cork lined caps
20	Bottles	39491	
21	Bottles, Antique	29797	Early Coke, Pepsi worth hundreds
22	Bowling, Vintage Items	159100	
23	Boxes, Ammunition	71131	
24	Breweriana	562	Caps, Cans, Advertising, Clothing
25	Building Toys	18998	Legos, Tinker Toys, Lincoln Logs
26	Buttons	41195	Look for Military, Character Buttons
27	Calculators, Vintage	58042	
28	Calendars	41183	
29	Calls, Duck Hunting	36252	Plus Goose, Turkey -good $
30	Candle Holders	4062	
31	Cards, Greeting	35889	Also sold for collages, crafts
32	Cards, Playing	1438	Can be sold as decks, or singles

33	Cartoons and Characters	1344	
34	Casino Collectibles	898	Chips, Dice, Advertising, Apparel
35	Cast Iron Items	3631	Table and Kitchen Items, Wall Decor, Toys
36	China, Dinnerware	24	Sets $$
37	Christian Items	11668	
38	Christmas Collectibles	13877	Very Abundant and Worth Good Money
39	Christmas Decorations	907	Ornaments, Decor, Nativities
40	Clocks	397	Even 1970s Alarm Clocks, Bakelite
41	Coasters	13907	Sets much better
42	Corals	165715	
43	Costume Jewelry, Beads	156281	
44	Crucifixes and Crosses	11669	
45	Decorative Collectibles	13777	Plates, Figurines, Curios, Baskets
46	Decoys, Hunting	71131	Early Duck decoys worth hundreds
47	Disney Items and Characters	137	Can be worth a lot of $
48	Drapes, Curtains	942	Vintage, retro Fabric
49	Dreidels	165694	

50	Fabric, Vintage	29817	Lengths of Vintage Fabric can be up to $800!
51	Fantasy, Magic Items	10860	Unicorns, Skulls, Gargoyles, Dragons
52	Fast Food Toys	19077	
53	Fishing Decoys, Spearing	793	Old carved decoys over $100
54	Fishing Items, Vintage	792	Fly Rods & Reels worth hundreds
55	Fishing Lures, Vintage	36169	Can be worth a lot of $$
56	Fishing Reels, Vintage	36175	Complete or Parts Easy to find, worth good $
57	Fishing Rods	11144	Vintage or not
58	Fishing Tackle Boxes	793	
59	Fishing Taxidermy	159028	Finished Mounts over $100, $50 for common
60	Fishing, Fly	23810	
61	Fishing, Vintage Items	792	
62	Flags and Pennants	13881	
63	Flashlights	13863	
64	Flies, Fishing	11142	
65	Football, Vintage Items	159120	
66	Fraternal Organizations	402	Scouts, Lions Club, Kiwanis, Knights

67	Frisbees	19017	
68	Games, Handheld Electronic	19072	Easy to find, older ones worth good $
69	Glass, 40s-60s	4207	Anchor-Hocking, US, Fenton
70	Glass, Art	955	
71	Glass, Carnival	2668	Fenton, IN Glass Cos.
72	Glass, Crackle	2712	
73	Glass, Depression	1002	Anchor Hocking, IN, US Glass
74	Glass, Pyrex	4765	
75	Glass, Vaseline	4935	Bright Yellow-Green Glass
76	Golf Balls, Vintage	18924	
77	Golf Club Head Covers	18930	
78	Golf Items, Vintage	83041	Balls, Bag Tags, Score Cards, Ads, Clothes
79	Greeting Cards, Vintage	35889	
80	Gun Parts, Vintage	71131	
81	Halloween Collectibles	14285	Can be worth more than you think
82	Halloween Items	907	Actually worth more than Christmas items!
83	Historical Items	13877	Police, Fire Depts, Organizations
84	Holiday Decorations	907	
85	Horse Shoes, Tossing Vintage	79790	For Horseshoes game - Can be $20 set

86	Hunting, Vintage Items	71131	
87	Insulators, Glass & Ceramic	795	Can be found near existing power lines
88	Jars, Cookie	4047	Character Jars VG
89	Jewelry, Vintage and Antique	48579	Brooches, too!
90	Jewish Items	13773	
91	Key Chains	38016	
92	Kitchen Items	81	Utensils, Canisters, Table Ware, Appliances
93	Kites	2569	
94	Knives	1401	Old Swiss Army Knives!
95	Lace and Doilies, Vintage	945	
96	Lamps, Electric	4053	
97	Lamps, Oil	4057	
98	Legos		Even newer Lego Sets, Men can be $30
99	Letters, Correspondences	156488	Love Letters, Military Letters
100	Lighters	951	Vintage Lighters can be worth $200+
101	Lunch Boxes and Thermoses	1409	Do not have to be Character boxes!
102	Magnets	476	

103	Maps and Atlases	37958	Can be worth good $
104	Maps, Vintage	1412	
105	Marbles	771	Can be big $ for old marbles
106	Maritime Antiques	37965	Bells, Anchors, Nets, Ship Items
107	Match Books	156496	
108	Medical, Dental Items	4065	
109	Menorahs	13775	
110	Menus, Restaurant	1437	
111	Militaria	13956	Especially Civil War and WW2 items
112	Models, Vintage	1188	Unassembled worth much more
113	Motorcycle Items	10958	
114	Mugs, Coffee	38148	
115	Music CDs, Records, Tapes	11233	Records and obscure CDs best
116	Napkins, Vintage	165662	Packs, Old
117	Napkins, Halloween		$30-50
118	Night Lights	157010	
119	Other Holiday Collectibles	907	St Patrick's Day, Valentines
120	Pens and Pencils	966	

121	Pentacles, Wicca	35835	
122	Perfumes and Perfume Items	35982	
123	Pewter Items	1434	
124	Pez Dispensers	4097	Look for items with no feet
125	Photographs, Vintage	14277	
126	Pin Cushions	1465	
127	Pins (Pin-backs)	50787	Look for Obscure Campaign Buttons
128	Plastic Retro Items	108962	Lucite, Lustro-Ware, Serving Pieces
129	Police Collectibles	928	Old Badges worth big $
130	Political Items	4100	Campaign Pins, Posters
131	Post Cards	914	
132	Pottery, Art	27	Can be worth a lot of $$
133	Print Advertisements	34	or Sell in Subject Matter's Category
134	Puzzles, Jigsaw	2613	Wood, Springbok Circular Puzzles VG
135	Quilts	947	
136	Radios, Vintage + Parts	931	Part out broken radios!
137	Retro, Vintage Items	69851	BAKELITE, Hippie, Mod Art pieces
138	Science Fiction and	152	Star Wars, Trek, X-Files,

	Horror		UFOs, Aliens
139	Sewing Items, Vintage	113	
140	Shakers, Salt and Pepper	4049	Characters, Should be Pair
141	Shells	82515	Sea Shells, Conches, Sand Dollars
142	Shot Glasses	3273	
143	Signs, Antique	63519	Ceramic, 2-Sided best
144	Silver-plate Items	1436	
145	Skateboarding Items	16262	
146	Skateboards	16264	
147	Skateboards, Vintage & Parts	114248	
148	Slot Cars	2616	
149	Souvenirs and Travel	165800	By State, Country -Spoons, Patches, Mugs
150	Spools, Thread		
151	Sports Cards	212	
152	Sports Memorabilia	50123	
153	Stamps	260	Can be attached to Envelopes
154	Swizzle Sticks, Vintage	10905	Bakelite, Metal Handles
155	Table Linens, Cloths	13954	
156	Tarot Cards	35837	

157	Telephones, Vintage + Parts	38036	Parts often worth more than the entire phones
158	Thermometers, Barometers	14020	
159	Thimbles	38060	
160	Tin Items	10950	Collectible Tin Containers
161	Tobacco Items	593	
162	Toleware Items, Decor	1218	Antique Painted, Floral
163	Tools	4121	Especially Planes, Old Saws, Farm Items
164	Tools, Vintage	4121	Esp. Skeleton Keys, Planes, Forged Tools
165	Toy Soldiers	2631	Don't have to be that old
166	Toys, Action Figures	246	
167	Toys, Antique	717	
168	Toys, Building	18991	Legos worth $, Tinker Toys, Lincoln Logs
169	Toys, Celluloid	722	From 40s, 50s - $20-100
170	Toys, Die Cast Vehicles	222	Matchbox, Hot Wheels cars, examples
171	Toys, Tin	735	
172	Toys, Wind-up	74986	
173	Train and Railroad Items	1444	
174	Traps, Animal	71131	Some old traps worth over

			$1000 Newhouse
175	Trivets	11656	
1776	Trucking and Semi Items	35976	
177	Tubes	64627	Can be worth $50 for matched pairs, quads
178	Tupperware	13934	
179	TV, Movie, Character Toys	2624	Look for popular 80s TV shows, movies
180	Vanity Collectibles	597	Hair Items, Shaving, Perfumes
181	Vintage Bicycles and Parts	35959	
182	Watches	14324	
183	Waterford Crystal / Glass	7291	
184	Weather Vanes and Balls	37918	Antique Iron -Worth $100s
185	Wicca and Pagan Items	35831	
186	Yo-Yos	2664	Duncan, old wood

APPENDIX 3: ORGANIC ITEMS

#	ITEM	CAT.	DESCRIPTION
1	Agates	3215	
2	Antlers, Sheds	71124, 4560	
3	Asparagus [Wild]	115722, Local Bus	
4	Basswood, Black Walnut, Ash Wood	160675	Cut to blocks for carving
5	Berries, [Wild]	25460	
6	Berries, Blackberries [Wild]	25460	
7	Berries, Cranberries [Wild]	25460	
8	Bones, Animal	45604, 36271, 1466	Taxidermy, Animal Collectors, More
9	Boughs, Pine & Cedar	Local Businesses	For Wreath Making, Holiday Crafts
10	Burls, Wood	3127	For Wood Carving, Turning. Can be $1000
11	Coral 169311 Aquariums	66793	
12	Cottonwood Bark	160675	For Carving - $20/8 pcs
13	Deer Tails	87096	Fly Tying

14	Driftwood	66789, 1285, 71130	Aquariums, Terrariums, Taxidermy, Signs
15	Eggs, Blown	116639	Empty Shells for Crafts -Ducks, Chicken, Goose
16	Feathers, Bird	45220, 41199	HOT for Hair Accessories, Colorful
17	Feathers, Duck	44913	Fly Tying
18	Feathers, Goose	41199	Domestic - For Blankets, Coats
19	Fossils	3215	
20	Fur, Other Animal	87096, 71130	Fly Tying - Woodchuck $3, Squirrel
21	Fur, Rabbit, Hare	87096	Fly Tying
22	Hives, Bees Hornets	71130	Taxidermy -MAKE SURE ITS EMPTY -$20
23	Horns, Bull	71130	Taxidermy
24	Leeks [Wild Onions]	115722, Local Bus.	
25	Meteorites, Tektites	3239	Meteorites can be worth $1000s
26	Mushrooms, Chanterelles	115722, Local Bus.	
27	Mushrooms, Morel	115722, Local Bus.	
28	Nuts, Pecans	25460	
29	Nuts, Walnuts	25460	
30	Petrified Wood	3215	
31	Pine Cones	103479	Crafts, Wreath Making

32	Rocks, Stones for Aquariums	66793	Holey Rocks up to $25 a piece
33	Sand Dollars	157016	
34	Sea Shells	82515, 116418	Sea Shell Collectibles, Aquarium
35	Sea Shells	82515	Large Conch Shells can be $20+
36	Skulls, Animal	45604	
37	Squirrel Tails	87096	Fly Tying, Lure Making
38	Star Fish	157019	
39	Stone, Petoskey 3215	3215	Up to $50 for Large -Polished or Rough
40	Stones, Beach / River Polished	66793	
41	Stones, Pudding	3215	
42	Wood Blanks for Turning	71235	Carving, Turning - Nice Grains
43	Wood Plaques 71130	71130	Background for Taxidermy- Cedar, Oak, Juniper

APPENDIX 4: USABLE ITEMS

#	ITEM	CAT.	DESCRIPTION
1	Air Conditioners, Parts	20711	Scrap - Lots of copper in old ACs
2	Archery Equipment 20835		Bows, Arrows, Shafts, Tabs, Guards
3	Audio / Video, Vintage and Parts	175740	
4	Baby Food Containers [glass, plastic]	57736	Used for craft supply storage
5	Baby Food Containers, Plastic + Lids	83893, 44912	Used for Beads, Fly-Making Supply Holders
6	Bar Items and Accessories	3265	Bar Sets, Corkscrews, Pitchers, Taps, etc
7	Bar Tools	20687	
8	Barn Doors and Hardware	162926	Vintage doors $300-800, Iron Hardware VG
9	Barn Wood	84011	Sold by board, or sell locally Craigslist
10	Baseball and Softball Gear	16021	
11	Batteries, Rechargeable	48619	Any batteries that work - Can be up to $40
12	Battery Compartment Covers	eBay	List in category of complete unit

13	BBQ Grill Tools	20725	
14	Beach Glass	41221	
15	Beads from Vintage Costume Jewelry	156281	Bakelite, colorful
16	Bells, Small to Medium	71110	Used for Hunting Dog Locators
17	Bike Accessories	22688	
18	Bike Parts, Newer Bikes	57262	
19	Bike Parts, Vintage	56197	Some worth quite a lot - Easier to part them out
20	Billiards / Pool Balls	75192	
21	Billiards Accessories	75184	Cues, Balls, Racks, Decor
22	Bird Houses	20502	Home Made VG
23	Board Game Parts, Dice, Pieces	7317	Check out everything you can sell here!
24	Board Games and Parts	233, Amazon	Pick up any Sealed games for Amazon
25	Book Dust Jackets, Illustrations	121833	Scrapbooking
26	Bottle Caps	160732	Scrapbooking, Crafts
27	Bottles, Wine	38172, CL	For Wine Making
28	Bowling Ball Bags, Vintage	169291	Sell for $10-50 as Women's Purses
29	Bowling Gear	20846	

30	Boxes [Empty]	eBay	Electronics Boxes can be worth $20!
31	Boxes [Empty] Small	83893, 44912	Fly, Bead Storage, Also for shipping Jewelry
32	Brass Bullet Shells [Empty]	SMD, CL	For Reloading, Scrap Value
33	Brass, Scrap	29402 SMD	
34	Building Toys Lots	18991	Esp. Legos -random lots
35	Butter Containers w/Lids [Empty]	eBay	Lots of 20 -Various categories
36	Cabinet Hardware	41971	Pulls, Slides, Hinges
37	Calls, Hunting	36252	Can be $50 - Sterilize and sell
38	Camping and Hiking Gear	16034	Vintage or Not
39	Candles	46782	Yankee Candle VG
40	Carbide Steel Scrap	29402, SMD	Drill Bits, tool ends, etc. Nice $$
41	Cases from Vintage Electronics	175741	Wood best, Audio Receiver Cases
42	Cases, Plastic [Empty]	eBay	Everybody wants these for storage, packaging
43	Caster Wheels, Vintage	162913	Sets of 4 if possible -$10-50
44	Catalytic Converters, Scrap	29402, SMD	From autos, worth $20-150

45	CD Cases [Empty]	307	
46	CD/DVD/Media Racks	22653	Easy to Find, Can be sold on Amazon
47	Chainsaw Parts	85915	Bars, Chains, Guards, Cases
48	Cigar Cases/Tubes [Empty]	156508	Cigar Display, also used for crafts
49	Clothing, Vintage	91235, 91244	Old Ties, Suits, Dresses = Big Bucks
50	Computer Board Gold Fingers	29402, SMD	Trim off w/wire cutters, shears
51	Computer Boxes	175690	Plus boxes for Accessories and Computers
52	CPUs Processors	164	Sold Single or lots, can be scrapped for good money
53	Computer Games, PC	175690	Floppy Disks, Cassettes, etc
54	Computer Motherboards	1244, e-Scrap Sites	Sold as replacements, or scrapped
55	Computer, Logos	175690	Emblems, etc -Old Apple, Commodore, etc
56	Computer, Manuals and Paperwork	175690	
57	Computer, Outer Cases	175690	
58	Computer, Software and Disks	175690	
59	Computers, Circuit Boards	175690	For Parts, Rebuilding Computers, or Scrap
60	Computers,	175690	Cords, Joysticks, Mice, Disk

	Components		Drives, etc
61	Computers, IC Chips	175690	Scrap for Gold, or Collectible - Some Big $
62	Computers, Memory	175690	Scrap Value, or for additional Mem for PCs
63	Computers, Parts	175690	
64	Computers, Vintage	171957	Working or Not
65	Containers, Prescription Drug	83893, 44912	57736 Used for Craft, Fly-Making Holders
66	Containers, Skin Care [Empty]	11862	Used for Making Travel Kits, Refills
67	Cookware	20628	Old Cast Iron items VG
68	Copper, Scrap	29402, SMD	
69	Cords, cables for Electronics	14961 AZ, SMD	
70	Corks, Wine	71177	For Crafts, Wine Making Get from Local Bars/Restaurants
71	Cornhole Toss Game Bags	79791	Easy to Make, Easy to Sell
72	Coupons	172010	
73	Coupons and Gift Cards	172008	
74	Croquet Items	117210	Vintage Balls $10, Wicket Sets $10, Posts, Mallets
75	Crosses, Decorative	75570	Altered Art, Collage,

			Steampunk Art
76	Darts, Dartboards	26328	
77	Decoys, Hunting	36249	If you see cheap decoys, buy them!
78	Decoys, Hunting Accessories	36249	Duck decoy anchors, hooks, lines
79	Dice	7317	Used for Crafts, Scrapbook, Jewelry
80	Dinnerware, Serving Pieces	36027	
81	Doll Parts	75570	Altered Art
82	Dominoes	2555	Collectible, or Mixed Lots used for Crafts
83	Door Hardware & Knobs	37911	Glass Knobs, Ornate Knobs VG
84	Door Hardware, Parts	41976	Knobs, Hinges, Locks, Handles, Locksets
85	DVD Cases [Empty]	617	
86	Eyeglass Frames	SMD	Vintage Frames were Gold-Filled
87	Fabric, Vintage	28162	Anything from old drapes, upholstery, etc
88	Fabrics, Vintage	38000	From Bolts, Furniture seats, Blankets, etc
89	Face Plates, Vintage Audio	175741	
90	Fasteners, Screws,	20600	

	Nails		
91	Feet, Vintage Electronics	14998	Cushioned Feet from Audio best
92	Film Containers - Empty 35mm	4201	Lots of 10+, also used for crafts, beads, flies
93	Fishing Accessories	72603	
94	Fishing Lures	31689, 36153	
95	Fishing Lures - Broken, Parts	165931	Especially from Vintage, Lips, Bodies
96	Fishing Lures, Empty Boxes	31689	
97	Fishing Pole Parts	62153	For Pole Repair, Building - Guides, Handles, Parts
98	Fishing Rod Guides, Handles, Parts	62153	Take from Broken Fishing Rods
99	Fishing Sinker Containers, Spinning	83893, 44912	Used for Beads, Fly-Making Supply Holders
100	Fishing, Fly	23810	High $ Items -Rods, Creels
101	Fishing, Freshwater	36145	
102	Fishing, Ice	36152	Can be worth more than regular fishing stuff
103	Fishing, Saltwater	23821	
104	Flash Cards, Number Cards	75570	Altered Art, Collage
105	Flatware, Silverware	20693	Older are Silver-plate, scrap

				value
106	Football Gear	21214		
107	Frames, Picture	21214		
108	Furniture Parts, Pieces	162913		Handles, Arms, Legs, Rails, Trim, etc
109	Garden Decor	20498		Chimes, Flags, Sun Dials, Water Items
110	Garden Supplies	2032		
111	Garden Tools	29515		
112	Gears and Cogs, Metal	75570		Altered Art, Steampunk
113	Gears, Sprockets	75570		For Altered Art, Collage Crafts
114	Glass, Polished and Smooth	163778		Beach polished better
115	Golf Balls	18924		Used lots, or vintage balls worth $
116	Golf Club Head covers	18930		
117	Golf Clubs	115280		Singles, or Sets -Drivers VG
118	Greeting Cards [Vintage]	121833		For Scrapbooking
119	Grill, Gas Parts	20724		Knobs, wheels, grills, elements, burners
120	Guitar Parts	159953		Part out broken guitars for good money
121	Guitars	159953		Complete or Broken can still sell
122	Gun Parts	73943		Magazines, Choke Tubes, Barrels easy to sell

123	Handles, Drawers & Cabinets	20601	Vintage, Glass, Brass
124	Handles, Plumbing Valve & Faucet	37911, 75570	Cast Iron, Aluminum
125	Heaters, Furnace Parts	41987	
126	Horse Shoes, Tossing	79790	Singles or Sets
127	Hunting Accessories	52502	
128	Hunting Clothing	36239	Camouflage clothing -Army Surplus
129	Hunting Knives	42574	
130	Hunting Reloading Supplies	31823	
131	Hunting Taxidermy	36271	Worth VG $ -Actually see this quite often at sales
132	Jelly Jars [Empty]	28114	Canning, Making Candles, Storage
133	Jewelry Costume	500	
134	Jewelry for Parts and Repair	168176	Can get good money for lots of broken jewelry!
135	Jewelry Pieces, Parts from Broken	164353, 168176	For Jewelry Making, Repair
136	Jewelry, Loose Beads	488	Can also sell beads from Old Furniture, Lamps here
137	Kitchen Tools, Gadgets	20635	
138	Knobs, Furniture Handles -Antique	20635	
139	Knobs, Vintage	14998	Especially from high-end

	Electronics		Audio -Bakelite
140	Lamp Parts and Pieces	13865	Filial, Knobs, Hanging Hardware can be Sold!
141	Lawn Mower Parts, Accessories	82248	Sell the Wheels, Seat, Blades before Scrapping!
142	Letter Tiles, Scrabble [Wooden]	19097, 71178	For Crafts, Scrapbooking, Lots of 100 best
143	Logos / Emblems	eBay	From old Electronics, Cars, Bikes, etc
144	Luggage and Travel Bags	16085	
145	Magazines	280	Print Ads, Articles may be worth more
146	Make-up and Accessories	31786	Includes Vintage Make-up
147	Manuals / Instructions	eBay	Sell in Vintage Electronics, or Item Category
148	Media, Blank	64627	Reel to Reel, Cassettes, All Kinds
149	Metal, Alloys, Scrap Metal	29402, SMD	
150	Microwave Parts	150138	Sell Glass Trays $20+, Magnetrons, Motors
151	Motors, Electric	175741	Can sell small Motors as Lot, or Lg Separate
152	Motors, Electric Scrap	29402, SMD	Also copper windings and breakage
153	Music CDs, Vinyl Records, Tapes	11233	Sell as singles or in lots
154	Musical Instruments, Brass & Parts	16212	Usually parts are better than Brass Scrap value
155	Nail Polish and	11871	Sell in Lots

	Accessories		
156	Nails, Square (Vintage)	162930	Crafts, Vintage Restorations
157	Number Tiles, Rummikub Game	7317	Used for crafts, scrapbooking
158	ORV Parts and Accessories	eBay Motors	
159	Outdoor Holiday Decor	117416	
160	Outdoor Power Equipment and Parts	29518	Blowers, Edgers, Weed Whips, Hedgers
161	Oven / Range Parts	43566	Knobs, Motors, Elements, Handles, Burners!
162	Oven Burners / Elements	43566	
163	Oven Racks	43566	$20-40 for good condition
164	Paint Brushes, Vintage	28110	
165	Paper Dolls and Clothing	75570	Altered Art, Collage
166	Patio Furniture Parts, Pillows	20716	
167	Perfumes and Colognes, Vintage	26396	Can be worth more than you would think
168	Photographs, Vintage	14277	
169	Ping Pong Paddles	36277	
170	Plumbing and Parts	20601	Parts or Scrap
171	Plumbing Fixtures,	167948	Antique Brass, Cast Iron,

	Handles, Faucets		Ceramics
172	Pool Toys	159921	
173	Portable Audio, Headphones	15052	Even vintage Walkman
174	Posters and Prints	41511	
175	Pottery Pieces, Shards	18875	
176	Power Strips, Surge Protectors	67779	Or scrap for copper value
177	Push-Up Pop Containers	102391	Used for Making Cupcake Shooters, Jell-O
178	Railroad Ties	Local, CL	For Landscaping
179	Recipes	20475	
180	Reel to Reel Tapes, Empty Spools	14998	VG
181	Refrigerator / Freezer Parts	71259	Handles, Racks $20-40, Drawers $20
182	Remote Controls, Electronic	eBay, AZ	Old Remotes can be worth $25+
183	Shoe Boxes, Vintage [Empty]	163628	Old Nike Boxes have been sold for $75!
184	Shoes, Vintage	163628, 74976	80s Tennis Shoes, Old Wing Tips Women Shoe
185	Shotgun Shell Boxes [Empty]	71116	Used for Reloading
186	Shotgun Shell Hulls [Empty]	Reloading Sites, CL	For Reloading and Christmas Lights!

187	Showerheads	71282	
188	Skateboard Parts	159073	
189	Skateboarding Clothing	159077	
190	Skateboards	16264	
191	Sleds and Tubes	59892	
192	Snow Plows and Parts	eBay Motors	Hoses, Lights, Control Pieces Easily Removable
193	Speakers, Vintage or Not	50597	Even emblems from Speakers worth $
194	Spikes, Railroad	95163	Used for Coat Hooks, Knife Handles
195	Spools, Empty 620 Film	167943	For Vintage Film reloading $7/Pc
196	Spools, Empty Thread, Wooden	14083	
197	Spools, Ribbon [Empty]	71224	
198	Spools, Wire [Empty]	100180	
199	Sporting Goods Equipment	382	
200	Sporting Goods, Used	159043	Almost anything has value if it works
201	Spray Dispensers [Empty]	1277	Used for Making Gift Baskets, Potpourri
202	Telephones and Parts	3286	Entire Phones, Batteries, Battery Doors
203	Tennis and Racquet Gear	159134	

#	Item	Code	Notes
204	Thermostats and Parts	115947	
205	Tools, Hand	3244	
206	Tools, Power	3247	
207	Tooth Brushes, Used	For You	Use for Cleaning Collectibles, Guns
208	Toy Parts	1198	Vintage Tonka, Metal Parts, Part out old toys!
209	Toys, Broken and Parts, Vintage	1198	Pieces & Parts of old toys, cars
210	Tractor, Agricultural Parts	160934	
211	Transformers, Power (electronics)	175741	
212	Traps, Animal	71108	Good $$
213	T-Shirts, Vintage	28022	Rock Concert Shirts, Character, TV Shows
214	Tubes, Cosmetics [Empty]	88433	Lotion Tubes, etc -Clean, $7 for 20
215	Tubes, Plastic	159046	Lidded, Used for Geocaches
216	Tubing, Aluminum, Copper, etc	29402, SMD	
217	Tupperware Containers	20625	Especially pre-1980s
218	Turntables for Records, and Parts	48649	
219	Turtle Shells	71129	
220	Typewriter Keys	75570	Old Flat Keys Best -Altered Art, Steampunk

#	Item	Code	Notes
221	Vacuum Parts, Vintage	42146	
222	Vehicle Air Cleaner Assemblies	EM	
223	Vehicle Body Parts	EM	Can lot of $
224	Vehicle Buttons, Controls	EM	From Radios, Heaters, Dials, Displays
225	Vehicle Catalytic Converters	EM, SMD	
226	Vehicle Cup Holders, Storage Acc.	EM	
227	Vehicle Floor Mats	EM	
228	Vehicle Gas Caps	EM	
229	Vehicle Gauges, Displays	EM	Can be VG from old cars
230	Vehicle Glove Box Doors	EM	
231	Vehicle Headlights and Rings	EM	Easily removable and sold
232	Vehicle Hub Caps, Rims	EM	
233	Vehicle Instrument Panels	EM	
234	Vehicle Interior Door Panels	EM	
235	Vehicle Interior Upholstery	EM	

236	Vehicle Light Bulbs, Ext & Int eBay Motors	EM	Can be good $ from working vintage lights
237	Vehicle Lighters	EM	Easily Lost and Sold
238	Vehicle Logos and Hood Ornaments	EM	Highly Collectible!
239	Vehicle Mirrors	EM	Easily Broken and Often Ordered from eBay
240	Vehicle Motor Parts	EM	Or scrap out the copper wires
241	Vehicle Parts, Vintage & Collectable	EM	Any salvageable parts from old car bodies can be sold
242	Vehicle Pedals and Pads	EM	
243	Vehicle Seat Belts	EM	Easily sold
244	Vehicle Spark Plug Wires	EM	Easily removable and sold
245	Vehicle Tire Caps	EM	Yes even these can be sold off old tires
246	Vehicle Towing Accessories	EM	Hitches, Balls, Wiring Harnesses, Receivers
247	Vehicle Trim and Chrome, Vintage	EM	
248	Vehicle Turn Signals & Light	EM	
249	Vehicle Visors	EM	Easily removable and sold
250	Vehicle Wheel Lug Nuts	EM	Single, or Sets are better
251	Vehicle Wiper Assemblies	EM	

252	Vehicle, Door / Window Handles	EM	
253	Vials, Centrifuge / Lab	159046	Used as Geocaches - 10/$8
254	Video Game Cases [Empty]	1249	Especially Newer Console, Portables Cases
255	Video Game System Parts, Cords	54968	For any console
256	Video Games	1249	
257	Wall Decor	38233	
258	Wall Decor, Metal Art	38233	Good Place to Sell Detector Finds, Metal Crafts
259	Wallpaper	42135	Even Vintage Rolls
260	Washers and Dryers Parts	71256	Handles, Belts, Motors - I've Seen Knobs for $15
270	Washers, 2.5"	79790	For Washer Toss Yard Game - Set 16 $10
280	Watch Faces	160645, 75570	For Beading, Altered Art
281	Watch, Clock Hands	75570	Altered Art
282	Watches and Parts	14324	
283	Wedding Items	11827	
284	Weed Whip Parts	71278	Guards, heads, hardware
285	Window Parts	63514	Finials, Tie-Backs, Rods, Hooks
286	Windows, Screens, Parts	20592	
287	Wine Charms	31591	Easy to make, Sell well
288	Wine Glass Holders	159901	

289	Winter Sports Gear	36259	Skiing, Snowshoe
290	Wiring, Cloth-Covered Copper	175741	Used for rebuilding Vintage Electronics
291	Yarn	36589	Especially vintage, with Label

GARAGE SALE SUPERSTAR

How to Make the Most Money Possible at your Garage Sale, Yard Sale, Rummage Sale, Estate Sale, or Tag Sale

Copyright, Legal Notice and Disclaimer:

This publication is protected under the US Copyright Act of 1976 and all other applicable international, federal, state and local laws, and all rights are reserved, including resale rights: you are not allowed to give or sell this Guide to anyone else.

Please note that much of this publication is based on personal experience and anecdotal evidence. Although the author and publisher have made every reasonable attempt to achieve complete accuracy of the content in this document, they assume no responsibility for errors or omissions. Also, you should use this information as you see fit, and at your own risk. Your particular situation may not be exactly suited to the examples illustrated here; in fact, it's likely that they won't be the same, and you should adjust your use of the information and recommendations accordingly.

Any trademarks, service marks, product names or named features are assumed to be the property of their respective owners, and are used only for reference. There is no implied endorsement if we use one of these terms.

Finally, use your head. Nothing in this Guide is intended to replace common sense, legal, medical or other professional advice, and is meant to inform and entertain the reader.

Copyright © 2012 Eric Michael. All rights reserved worldwide

Almost Free Money

ISBN: 978-1482554960

INTRODUCTION

Welcome to the fun and exciting world of Almost Free Money. This is the second book in our successful series of e-books written to assist people in making more money at garage sales, yard sales, and second-hand stores.

In the first book in the series 'Almost Free Money', I discussed different avenues for making money on items that are available in most areas for free, or under $1. I discussed locating items at second-hand locations, such as garage sales, yard sales, thrift stores and flea markets, as well as places where you can find materials to sell for free while you recreate. I also gave readers detailed instruction on how to sell such items online, or at physical locations like garage sales and scrap metal sealers.

In this, the second book in the Almost Free Money series, we will discuss making "almost free" money by selling your property at free venues like garage sales, yard sales, estate sales, and tag sales. As a veteran of visiting over 1,000 garage sales in the last ten years, I can provide specific examples of what works for garage sale hosts, and what does not. I also have a background as a garage sale investor. I have been buying items at garage sales, and flipping them on eBay and Amazon for over twelve years. I can tell you what "flippers" are looking for, and how that can benefit you. You will earn how to advertise to all garage sale shoppers including flippers. We will discuss how to make the most money at your next garage sale by efficiently advertising and promoting your garage sale, so that hundreds of people will be lining up at your garage sale. You will learn how to effectively price your garage sale items, so that you get the most money possible without giving your customers sticker-shock.

I will also talk about the best way to organize your garage sale and lay out your displays and tables, so that you sell the most items and make the most money, while clearing out some of the clutter from your home. We will go over the best days to hold your garage sale or yard sale, and how long your sale should be open to maximize profit.

Garage Sale Superstar is leveraged with the background knowledge of the owners of Garage Sale Academy.com, a diverse website dedicated to assisting garage sale hosts in managing their garage sales and increasing profits.

I will also review several excellent sources to advance your knowledge base with further reading on the internet and there are several affordable opportunities to further your research and take the next step toward making your annual garage sale into a new business venture.

GENERAL INFORMATION

There are many areas that can affect the bottom line of your garage sale:

1. The Starting Time and Ending Time of your Sale
2. The Days of the Week that you are Open
3. The Time of Year for your Sale
4. The Organization of your Sale and Tables
5. Advertisement of your Sale
6. **Garage Sale Signs**
7. The Location of your Yard Sale
8. The Content of your Items
9. **Garage Sale Pricing**
10. Dealing with Customers

We will discuss all of these important aspects of your garage sale in detail in the following chapters.

GARAGE SALE AND YARD SALE TIPS

Let's start with some garage sales tips that will help you to make the most money from your potential garage sales items:

- Before you even start looking for stuff to sell, contact your neighbors, friends and relatives and decide on a weekend at least one month in the future that will work the best for everyone. Not everybody needs to be a cashier / host at the sale, but they will at least need to have their items priced and at the sale location. Multi-family garage sales will attract more shoppers and make you more money every time. The larger your sale is, the more customers you will get, and the more stuff you will sell. We will discuss multi-family garage sales more in-depth later.

- Holding your garage sale weeks in the future is great for several reasons. It allows you time to go through all your storage areas to find items to sell. Go through your attic, crawl space, garage, closets, and sheds to find stuff to sell. Go through the boxes that nobody has been into in years. You may have garage sale gold in those boxes! Also check all of your dresser drawers for clothes that are not worn anymore or kids' clothes that don't fit. Clothes make excellent money at garage sales, especially name brand items.

- Make a general list of the large high money items that you intend to sell at your garage sale, and have your co-hosts do the same. Compile one list for the sale that contains all of your big-ticket items so that you can include those items in your classified ads and online advertisements.

- Advertise your garage sale for TWO weeks before your sale, not just the prior week. Be creative with the title of your sale. Come up with a cool theme - 'Manly Garage Sale', 'Moms and Tots Sale', and 'Sportsperson's Yard Sale' are examples. We will cover advertisement along with additional garage sale tips in detail later.

- Check your garage sale inventory for items that will make you more money on eBay or Amazon. If you have never sold on these internet sites, don't be nervous! They both have exceptional instructions for getting started that any 12-year old can follow. You just have to go for it! Media items, collectible items, and designed clothes are areas where you will make significantly more money on the internet than at a garage sale!

For additional information on de-cluttering your home, another excellent source of information is my friend's Kindle book "Secrets of Quick Decluttering, Selling and Organizing the Home Area: Essential Step by Step Methods to Clutter-Free Lifestyle at Home & Earn Money through Selling Cluttered Items On eBay & Amazon"

GARAGE SALE ORGANIZATION

Organizing a garage sale is a free way to make significantly more money at your garage sale. You would think that every garage sale host would be organizing a garage sale to make the most money, wouldn't you? Common sense should tell you that if your yard sale looks good, and if the best items are closest to the customer's reach, that you would end up making more money. Yet, how many garage sales have you been to where stuff was strewn across tables, clothes are pulled off hangers, stuff is out of sight in boxes, and items are not even priced? I have seen hundreds of yard sales like I just described. Do you know how much stuff I bought at those sales...? Very little.

Here are some tasks that should be done before your garage sale is to be held:

1. Check out the chapters on getting ready for organizing a garage sale, yard sale, tag sale, or estate sale: **Garage Sale Tips**, **Garage Sale Advertising**, and **Garage Sale Signs**.

2. Organizing a garage sale should not be a one-person chore. Assign co-hosts to complete tasks - advertising, making signs, rounding up display materials, checking to see if there are garage sale sign, sale permit, or parking regulations where you live, getting change, and arranging for babysitters. There's plenty to do for everybody!

3. Get all of your garage sale items in one place several days ahead of time. Figure out how much volume you have, how many tables you will need and get everything priced BEFORE THE SALE. If your garage sale starts with un-priced items, you may not get time to get stickers on them, and most will go unsold.

4. After you get an idea of your volume, figure out what you will need for tables and displays. Find yourself a table and chairs for a check-out table. If possible, set up your tables and clotheslines the day before. Figure out where you will have people park their vehicles. Organizing a garage sale is easier after planning.

5. Get at least $50 in change. You will need at least $20 in one-dollar bills, and $5 in quarters. Decide who will collect money and give that person a money apron or fanny pack, so that the money is NOT sitting on a table in a box.

6. Round up an extension cord or two, (so you can test electric items, and run your fan for comfort, if it is hot). You may also want a supply of batteries for testing battery-powered items. Do not give away your good batteries inside sold items. They are expensive!

7. Call your co-hosts and make sure that everybody is still going to be there for the sale, and who is bringing what. You don't want any surprises the morning of your sale. Make sure that someone brings the coffee and doughnuts, and that somebody has arranged for lunch and cold drinks, if it is hot!

There is also plenty of organization work to do on the morning of your garage sale:

- Get there early! You do not want to be scrambling around at the last second, or even worse, organizing a garage sale after the sale has already started.

- Set up all tables and displays that you could not set up the night before. Make sure that everything is priced. Get everything out of boxes, so customers can see your items. Don't make your customers dig through your gross boxes.

- Have your co-hosts handle some tasks. One person should be handling the money. One person can greet people and answer questions (and perform kid-duty, if required). If you have additional support (sounds like a military recon, doesn't it?) have somebody assigned to organization. This is very important to your sales.

The Organization person should be keeping your sale looking good. Think of your yard sale like a clothing store. Make your shelves and tables look sharp. Keep moving items closer to the customers when stuff gets pushed to the back of the tables. Make sure clothes are spaced on your lines, and not falling off of hangers. Check to see that your items are not getting mixed in with other categories of items. Make sure toys are not on the ground where people can trip on them. Make sure that stacked items are not going to tip over and that your aisles are spaced correctly.

Ten tips for effective organization and spacing of your garage sale and yard sale tables, displays, and traffic flow:

1. Make sure that tables and displays are spaced out far enough that people are not bumping each other, or tripping each other. Make sure there is nothing on the ground that people could trip over or slip on when organizing a garage sale.

2. If at all possible, make your tables line up in straight lines, and make them the same height (waist-high tables for adults work well). Organize you tables so there is an obvious flow. Try to keep people moving in the same direction, as much as possible.

3. Put your large items and expensive items so that people see them when they first get to your sale.

4. Put your pay table at the front of your sale, and have a greeter to say hello to people. Customers will spend more money if they feel comfortable. They will also be more likely to buy stuff from you if they like you.

5. Make sure that your higher priced items are closer to the front of the tables, so people see them first.

6. Make sure people can reach all of your items, even little old ladies and kids. Keep toys where kids can see them and reach them. If you want to sell some toys, make sure kids at your sale can pick them up and play with them.

7. Run a clothesline inside your garage, and hang up tops, jackets, suits, dresses and all name brand clothing. It's OK to keep T-Shirts, shorts, and kids clothes folded up tables.

8. If you run short on tables, you can make tables from sawhorses or stacked boxes with wood paneling on top. Make sure you cover them all with clean sheets or table cloths.

9. When items sell, move unsold items from the backs of the tables to the fronts, where people can see them better. Space items out more, so there are not large gaps. Later, take down tables to make your sale look like it has more stuff.

10. When your garage sale is winding down, lower your prices and start offering deals! You don't want to clean up all that stuff, do you?

GARAGE SALE ADVERTISING

Garage sale advertising can effectively double the traffic to your sale. Free classifieds, Craigslist, and newspaper classifieds are options available to hosts. Speaking from the perspective of a long-time garage sale picker, I will tell you that 90% of the thousands of garage sales and yard sales that I have been to were found either on classified ads or online classified sites.

What does that mean for you, the garage sale host? You can't rely on simply throwing up a couple of rummage sale signs, if you want to get good traffic to your site. Sure, you will get a few shoppers, but you are holding the garage sale to make some money, and organize your home, so make the effort to advertise your garage sale. You can advertise garage sales for free. Here are some general advertising tips to help you get the most out of your advertising, and people to your sale:

1. Take advantage of listing your garage sale in free classified ads for two weeks prior to your sale, not just one week. Many newspaper classifieds are received on Wednesday or Thursday, and the extra week allows those people who don't immediately browse their classifieds to find your yard sale.

2. Garage sale ads should be posted in multiple locations, both online and in newspapers. It does not take very long to make an online classified listing for your garage sale on Craigslist and in your local 'Home Shopper' classified newspaper.

3. Make sure that you list your sale on Craigslist. Most garage sale pickers start planning garage sales routes by finding good sales to visit on Craigslist these days.

4. Garage sale signs are for navigation to your sale, not garage sale advertisement! Make sure your signs are visible from the roadway, so that customers can find their way to your sale. Do not rely on signs to bring in a high volume of traffic.

I will tell you exactly what I look for when using online and newspaper classified ads to select garage sales to visit during garage sale picking routes. In perusing hundreds, maybe thousands of yard sale ads, I am constantly surprised by how poorly worded many ads are that are in the classifieds. It is not rocket science. This is what your garage sale classified ad should contain:

- The particulars. Clearly state the **days of the week and dates** that your sale will be open, the **Times that your sale starts and ends**, and the **address**. That should be the first line. You may wish to add the closest main intersection, but most people either have GPS, or can use MapQuest on their cell phones these days.

- If other families are contributing to your sale, list your sale as a **'Multi-Family Garage Sale'**, or **'Neighborhood' Garage Sale**. It gives the impression that you will have lots of good swag at your sale. The other families do not all have be physically present at your site. If they gave you some stuff to sell, that's good enough for me.

- Descriptions that include phrases like **'years of accumulation'**, **'1st sale in years**!', and 'Grandma's first ever garage sale' would pique my interest. How about yours?

- List some interesting **items that will be for sale** at your garage sale. Garage sale advertising really should not be any different than a sales pitch at a department store. Make people interested in going to your sale. What are people looking for that you can use to get them to your sale? Collectibles, Sports Cards, Vinyl Records, Good Furniture, Baby and Kids Clothes, Toys, Old Books, Sporting Goods, Hunting and Fishing Gear, and Name-Brand women's clothes are several particulars that will bring in customers. Also list large **high-value items** like newer electronics, bicycles, lawnmowers, outdoor play sets, large collections like stamp collections and music collections.

- Specify whether you allow **'Early-bird Sales'**. You have to understand that even if you started your sale at 5AM, you would still have a couple of die-hards there are 4:30. Early-birds can be good for getting a jump-start on your sales, but often, hosts are still trying to get their sale set up, and dealing with taking money and answering questions from these people can be annoying. I've always thought that it was inconsiderate of the early-birds anyway. I never go to yard sales before the start time, for that reason.

The following is an example of a free garage sale advertisement at a free yard sale classifieds site like Craigslist. I honestly don't see any need to pay for classified ads anymore, with the exposure that you get with Craigslist garage sale ads. Take your money and put it into good yard sale signs and garage sale price stickers instead. Garage sale advertising can be done for free!

"5-Family Neighborhood Garage Sale. 5525 St. Joseph Street in Montcalm. Friday May 4 and Saturday May 5. Sale Open 7AM-3PM. NO EARLY SALES. Large accumulation, 1st sale at this address! Collectibles, Big-screen TV, CD'S & records, Food Processor, fishing gear, duck decoys, lots of man stuff & tools, women's name brand clothes, kids clothes & Toys. Holiday decorations. See you here!"

GARAGE SALE DAYS OF THE WEEK

As veteran garage sale hosts, we can give you good advice on which days you should be open. Should your yard sale be open only on Saturday, or on Friday and Sunday, too? What are the best garage sales days? We have been to hundreds of garage sales, and hosted many more. We can tell you what works, and what is just wasted time.

Saturdays are BY FAR the best garage sale days to be open. On busy weekends, you can make 60-70% of your garage sale money between 8AM and noon on Saturday. So, what does that tell us? #1, you had better be open for business between 8AM and 12 Noon on Saturday. #2, all of the other days only make up less than 30% of your sales, if you consider that you will probably make some additional good sales on Saturday afternoon past the 60-70% prime time period on Saturday morning.

Here are some other things to consider when deciding which garage sale days to be open:

- Saturdays are MUST-DO days for garage sales. You MUST be open early on Saturday mornings, and be open through mid-afternoon on Saturday, at a minimum. Obviously, the longer you are open and the more days you can stay open, the more sales you are going to have.

- Fridays are also good days for garage sales and yard sales. You should at least have you rummage sale open for half of a day, on Friday afternoon.

- You will get some of the really good customers on Friday, including the hard-core pickers and collectors. If you have many collectible items or expensive items to sell, make sure that you are open on Friday!

- Fridays can also allow you to try selling some of your more expensive items for higher prices. Try putting your max price on these items for a while on Friday. If they don't sell Friday, lower your prices a bit on Saturday morning.

- Sundays are poor days for holding yard sales. Many people go to church on Sunday mornings, and others gather for Sunday brunch or other meals. There is generally very poor traffic on Sundays. There is also a perception that all of the good stuff at garage sales is gone, only leaving picked-through trash.

- You may want to try to hold your garage sale around the first and third weekends of the months, when people often receive their paychecks. People also generally pay bills at the end of the month, so get them at the beginning of the month when they still feel like they can spend money your sale.

GARAGE SALE START TIME AND HOURS

When is the best garage sale start time? When is the best time to start a yard sale?

Even experienced garage sale hosts struggle with these questions. This is probably because there is no absolute right answer for a garage sale start time. If you click on the prior link, you will see some suggestions for maximizing your sales by being open at the right time on Funtime.com.

After holding and shopping hundreds of garage sales, yard sales, rummage sales, and estate sales, I will throw in my two cents on what your garage sale hours should be. I will discuss what time is best to start your garage sale, when to end your garage sale.

WHEN TO START YOUR GARAGE SALE

Your garage sale start time can be affected by several things, including the time of year you hold your sale, and where you live. If you live in hotter climates, you will want to take advantage of the cooler weather in the morning and start earlier. For the same reason, if you hold your sale in August when it is usually sweltering hot, start earlier.

Here are some general guidelines for when to start your sale:

1. Never start your sale after 9AM. Never! Most veteran garage sale pickers start garage sailing at 7AM, and are stopping for brunch by 10AM. Starting your yard sale after 9AM tells customers that you don't care much about your sale. I never go to sales that start after 9.

2. The earlier you can start your sale, the more sales you will get! The early bird gets the worm, and many senior citizen shoppers are up and out of the house by 6AM. Start your sale at 7AM and you WILL get some early sales, plus if you are the first sale open in your area, the majority of the veteran pickers will be at your sale first! This is especially true if you took my advice about garage sale advertising and listed a bunch of enticing items in your classified ad or Craigslist garage sale ad that collectors would be interested in buying from you.

3. Make sure you address EARLY BIRD shoppers. These are the people that show up at your house an hour before your listed garage sale start time. While annoying, these people often buy multiple items from garage sales. You can jump start your sales,

and still address these people by putting up a large sign that says "ALL SALES BEFORE 7AM (or your start time) ARE DOUBLE STICKER PRICE. Make sure you stick to that policy, even ten minutes before your start time.

4. Make sure that you have **prices** on all of your items BEFORE your yard sale starts, preferably the night before, so that you are not running around like a chicken with your head cut off when your garage sale starts

5. What about selling coffee and donuts at your sale? Everybody loves coffee and donuts, and a lot of people don't bother getting breakfast before they leave.

GARAGE SALE SIGNS AND STICKERS

Garage sale signs and yard sale signs are vital to your bottom line. Sign design and placement are two of the most important concerns. Often, your signs alone will bring people into your sale.

Make sure that people driving by your signs can read the most important information. If you are a garage sale shopper, you know how annoying it is to try to read the information on tiny garage sale signs with small print from a moving vehicle. Do you turn your car around or back up to re-read those signs? No. You just keep on going and look for the next sale.

How do you avoid that same fate when placing your own signs?

SIGN SIZE AND DESIGN

Make your yard sale signs legible! I cannot state this any more clearly. You MUST be able to read the writing on the signs from a moving car from at least 30-50 yards away, or else your signs are worthless. Do you think the average person can read thin ink writing on a standard piece of notebook paper from a moving car? Heck no. So why do so many yard sale hosts make their signs like that?

Your sign should be at least 12 x 18", and you should make them larger, if possible. Just be careful making them TOO large, as oversized signs can be easily folded over by the wind. Some municipalities and areas limit the size of signs - I have seen 2 x 2', or 4' square. Check your cities laws before making your signs.

The print on the sign is also important. The lettering on the sign should be in legible BLOCK LETTERING, and should be BLACK, not multi-colored. Black writing is the easiest to read. You should use the largest marker that you can find, or flat black paint. The background should be a light color, so that the black writing contrasts.

Put only the information that is necessary to get people to your sale on your signs, no distracting drawings or writing. Anything that takes people's eyes away from how to get to your sale is unnecessary. Balloons and streamers are also extraneous.

Garage sale signs must relay ONLY THREE IMPORTANT DETAILS:

1. Your Street Address

2. Time and days that you sale is Open

3. What kind of sale is it?

Make sure that your days and time are large enough to be read from a distance. Do not make 'garage sale' huge and the rest of the information tiny. You also want to make sure that your letters are not mushed together, making them difficult to read. Don't use dates, so that you can reuse your signs in future years.

SIGN CONSTRUCTION

If you're willing to buy pre-constructed yard sale signs, there are definite benefits, provided you buy the largest signs, as explained previously. Professional-looking signs send several messages to prospective garage salers.

- You care about your sale.

- You are likely to have quality items to buy, because you have the money to buy quality signs

If you do buy signs, make sure that they are made of thick stock, and that the posts or frames are sturdy enough to not get destroyed by a rainstorm and can be re-used for future sales.

If you decide to make your own signs, make sure that you use materials that are weather-resistant. Paper gets destroyed by rain, almost instantly. Cardboard is a bit better, but still melts in the rain. Poster-Board is fairly reliable, but may get folded by the wind. Corrugated plastic is the best option, but can get expensive if you place the correct number of signs. I usually use poster board, and use wood posts on both sides of the signs. Make sure the bottoms are tapered so that you can drive them into the ground easily.

If you use single sided poster board, only write on one side to prevent the bleed-through effect.

Where you put your garage sale signs is almost as important as what your signs look like. The more signs that you have out, the more customers you will pull in. At a minimum, you should have signs at the nearest high-traffic intersections. You should have several signs at each intersection, so that drivers can see your signs from each direction.

If your signs are more than a mile from your road, make sure you keep drivers on the route by making small signs with arrows and your address. Make doubly sure that there is a very visible sign at the last corner before your house, so that customers do not miss your road.

GARAGE SALE STICKERS

One of my pet peeves is yard sale hosts who are too lazy to put price tags on their used items. I hate it. I usually turn around and walk right back to my car, and I know that I am not the only one who feels that way. Unless you have a large box of similar items like books or CDs, each individual item should have a large price sticker on it. The price should be clearly marked on the side of the item that is visible to the shopper. The more obvious the price sticker is, the more likely a customer is to buy it, if the price is right.

Be careful putting price stickers on collectible items like music records and posters. It's a shame to damage items by putting gaudy stickers on the collectible portions. Put price stickers somewhere that it will not damage the item when the sticker is peeled off.

There are a number of important advantages to using sharp-looking manufactured yard sale stickers, like the ones seen above left. Here are some considerations:

- The faster you can price your garage sale items, the more time you have to find more stuff to sell. Time is money! It's more than twice as fast to peel and stick manufactured price stickers than to make your own price stickers.

- Manufactured yard sale labels look better, and the better and more organized your garage sale is, the more likely it is that people will feel good about buying your stuff. Make your sale look good!

- Color coding of price stickers allows rummage sale hosts to easily keep track of multiple family's sales, sales in multiple categories (red for books, green for music, etc.), and you could even use a certain colored sticker for items leftover from prior garage sales that you are still trying to get rid of.

- Price stickers are cheap. You really are not saving much money by using good price stickers rather than a roll of tape and an ink pen.

- Now with the ease of ordering labels online, you can order in two minutes and have labels delivered right to your house. You don't even have to go to the store to get them!

- Manufactured Garage Sale Stickers are highly visible. Customers that can see item prices easily are much more likely to pick up and buy an item that is for sale than an item that has the price sticker obscured.

- Manufactured price stickers are safer on collectible items than sticking masking tape on them, or (God forbid!) actually writing on the items with a marker. Try to avoid sticking ANY stickers on the dust jackets of books, especially antiquarian books. Stick your labels inside the book on the blank interior page, or better yet, use a chart like the one in the photo above and to the right to avoid putting stickers on books. You also want to avoid putting stickers on vinyl record jackets, collectible posters, and anything else that is antique and made of paper or cardboard. Think of your customers who are collectors when you are pricing your items!

GARAGE SALE PRICING

Garage sale pricing is the most vital factor in determining profits, and how much clutter you will get rid of! The challenge in yard sale pricing is to make the most money possible, while not frustrating customers pricing garage sale items higher than what they are used to seeing at typical garage sales and yard sales.

The fact that you are taking the time to read this e-book shows that you are in the upper 10% of garage sale hosts. You are making the extra effort to do some research into improving your yard sale. I can't tell you how many sales that I have been to where it is obvious that the host has put no thought or effort into their sale. Half of their items are not priced. There are full boxes lying all over the place. Half of the time, I can't even tell what is for sale, and what is not. Don't be one of these people!

It's important to adjust your garage sales prices to reflect the condition of your items. Make sure that mechanical items work, and items have all of their pieces. Don't offer items for full price, if they are worn. Don't try to make an extra dollar at the expense of your customer, if you know the item is not fully functional. Price those items to move. Make your money on collectibles, media items, and good quality kids and women's clothes. I will tell you that if I get to a sale and I see a bunch of overpriced items, I usually leave. I don't waste time haggling. It is an excellent idea to visit a number of garage sales to see what other hosts are using for garage sale prices on commonly sold items, so you know the ball-park that you should be starting in for your own garage sale pricing. We have also provided a fairly large list of commonly sold items and their average prices sold for at garage and yard sales in our Garage Sale Price Guide.

GARAGE SALE PRICING GUIDE

This Garage Sale Pricing Guide is a garage sale and yard sale price list of many commonly sold garage sales items. The prices shown are average prices from around the country, for items that are in average used condition. If you live in an upscale neighborhood, you may wish to raise prices 20% from the values provided.

A general rule of thumb is to reduce your price by 20-30% from the buy price listed on the garage sale pricing guide for each year that you own consumer electronics like TVs, computers, video game systems, etc. You should also take at least 50% off of the listed price for items that have major flaws like missing pieces, chipped glass, cracked plastic, missing power cords, missing CD and video game cases, etc.

These prices listed in the garage sale pricing guide are determined by going to thousands of garage sales, and buying these used items for reselling on eBay or for personal use. This is a sampling of items, to give you an idea of where to start for your garage sale pricing or yard sale pricing.

Media Items

Hardcover Books - $1-2 - Check all pre-1950 books, coffee table books, and newer texts on Amazon

Softcover Books - .25 or 5 for $1 Check all newer texts on Amazon.

Audio Books / CD Books - $1

Music CDs: - $1, unless rare. Sell in Bulk lots.

Vinyl Records: .25 - .50 for commons, $1+ for Rock, Blues, and Cult Soundtracks - Check records before selling. 45 RPMS generally less

Cassette Tapes / 8 Tracks: .25-.50 - Better to list in bulk for $5-10. Limited demand.

CD Storage Racks, Spinners: $3-10+ These sell for $20-50 on Amazon for large 100CD units!

DVDs - $1 for older to $5 for newer titles

Clothes

Kids Clothes - $1, $3-5 for Name Brands

Baby Clothes - $1-3

Women's Tops - $1-5

Men's Tops - $1-3

Name Brand Jeans - $5-10

Other Jeans - $1-3

Sweaters - $3-5

T-Shirts - .50 - $1

Tennis Shoes - $1-5, more for newer Nikes, etc.

Dress Shoes - $1-3

Women Shoes - $1-20, vary greatly by maker

Jackets, Outerwear - $3-10

Suits - $10 for outdated, to $50 for newer

Snow Boots - $1 for older, to $10 for good newer.

Household Items

Kitchen Appliances - $3-10

Dishes - Sets $10, individual 0.25-.50

Tupperware - 0.25 - $1 for large

Flatware - Sell in lots $1-3

Serving Dishes - $1

Good Pots, Pans 0.50 -$1

Wall Decor, Framed Art - $1-5, small. $5-10 Lg

Large Appliances - $25-50 (Fridges, ovens, etc. that work

Microwaves - $5-20

Picture Frames, Mirrors - 0.25 - $1

General Household - $1

Collectibles

Avon, Homco, small Knick-Knacks: $1

Collectibles Plates $.50 - $1

Pottery - $1-5

Longaberger Baskets - $3-10, more for older

Swarovski Crystals - $5-20 for large

Beer / Food Collectibles - $1-5

Collectible Prints - $5-10

Sports Cards - Check eBay

Sports Memorabilia - Check eBay

Entertainment Memorabilia - Check eBay

Video Games & Systems

Newer Video Games (PS3, Xbox 360, Wii, Dreamcast) - Check Amazon for prices, they vary greatly. Popular titles at least $10-20.

Video Games 5+ Years Old (PS2, Xbox 1, Game Cube, Super NES, Etc. - $1-3

Outdated Video Games (PS1, Sega Genesis, Nintendo 64) - .50 -$2, Classic games $5

Classic Video Games (Nintendo NES, Atari 2600, 400, 800, Colecovision, Intellivision) - $2-4, check all of these games, some are worth over $100!

Video Game Systems: Always sell for more on eBay or Amazon. Do not sell these at garage sales, unless you need immediate money.

Minimum for systems with no games: PS3, Xbox 360 $100, Wii $60, Classics $40-50, Outdated $20-30, 5+ $30-40. Newer handheld $40-60, older $20.

Newer Controllers: $5-15 (PS3 are $40 new)

Older Controllers: $1-2

Power Cords, AV cords, Remotes, etc.: $1

Toys and Games

Board Games - 0.50 - $2, more for electronic, and some newer high-end games.

Legos, Building Sets - These can bring big $$ on the internet. $5 for small lots, up to $20 for large

Handheld Electronic Games - $.25-$1

Barbie Dolls - Older can be highly collectible. Newer $1-3, clothes, accessories $.25-$5 for vehicles.

Stuffed Animals, Dolls - $.25-$1 for high-end

Action Figures - .25 -$1, Transformers $1 small, up to $10 for large new figures

Hot Wheels, Matchbox Vehicles: Some are highly collectible. Newer - Sell in lots 10/$1

Vintage Toys - $1-5

General Toys - .25

Holiday / Christmas

Ornaments - .25-$1, Hallmark Keepsakes in box $1-5 for collectibles like

Star Wars, Wizard of Oz, etc.

Vintage Ornaments - $.50-$2

Artificial Xmas Trees - $10-40

Lights - .25-$1.00, depends on length

General Xmas Decor - $.50 - $2

Halloween Costumes - $1-10 for newer popular

Outdoors

Power Tools - $5-20 for working with batteries

Power Tool Batteries, Chargers - $2-5 for newer

Lawn Mowers (Push) - $10-20

Lawn Mowers (Riding) - $30 minimum

Bikes - $5-10 for kids, average. Check eBay for high-end bike prices

Sports Equipment -$1-5

Fishing Poles - $1 Cheap to $10 for name brand and large Salt Water, Salmon Rods

Fishing Tackle - $5-20 for full boxes

Small Landscaping, Garden Tools -$.50-$2

Long Handled Tools- (Rakes, Shovels, etc.) - $2-5

Small Tools -(Screwdrivers, Hammers, etc.) 0.50 -$1

Pet Supplies - 0.50 - $2

AFTER YOUR GARAGE SALE: GETTING RID OF YOUR STUFF FOR FREE

After your garage sale is over, what do you do with all of the unsold items? There are still ways for you to make money on your unsold items!

Well, I'll tell what you do NOT want to do! Do NOT pack the stuff back up and put it back into your house, storage shed or barn. You want to GET RID OF THE STUFF. That is why you have a garage sale in the first place. So... how do we accomplish the task, and maybe make a little bit of money on your leftover stuff?

Here are some options for garage sale, yard sale, rummage sale, and estate sale hosts for garage sale cleanup:

1. DO NOT PAY MONEY FOR GARAGE SALE CLEAN-UP. There are many ways to avoid this. There are many people advertising on Craigslist that will pick up your leftover stuff for free. You can also set boxes at the road with a FREE sign. Somebody will pick up the boxes.

2. Re-Check everything you have left after the garage sale for items that you can sell online (or somebody else you know can sell it, if you don't want to). Most media items can be sold online on eBay or Amazon.

3. Keep stuff together by category. If you have boxes full of books, music, holiday decor, name brand clothing, etc., make a quick

listing on Craigslist, and tell people you have a large lot of whatever you have for $5. Somebody will buy it.

4. You can take boxes of books to Used Book stores and get something for them. Take boxes of CDs or records to used music shops.

5. Another excellent idea is to coordinate with another future garage sale hosts. Is your neighbor going to have a large garage sale in a couple of weeks? When is your local community or church sale? See if you can drop off your good leftover items for their sale! You may have to help with set-up or something, but it is worth it.

6. Most cities have a Boy Scout or other organizational benefit at some point in the summer. You can drop off boxes of stuff for them to sell and claim a donation on your income taxes. See below.

7. BEFORE YOU THROW STUFF IN THE TRASH, YOU CAN WRITE OFF USED ITEMS DONATED TO CHARITY FOR EXCELLENT INCOME TAX WRITE-OFFS. Check **Itsdeductible.com** for a large list of IRS-approved, acceptable donation amounts for commonly donated items. You will be very surprised at how much you can write off! It's is definitely worth the time it takes to register on the site, and make your list of items for donation. Make sure that you take digital photos of the boxes and items for your tax records.

YARD SALE TIPS

Here are some yard sale tips to help you make the most money at your sale this year!

1. When you hold a garage sale, you are primarily protected inside of your garage. Yard sale hosts have to account for the weather. Make sure that you have a Rain Date in your advertisements, usually the following weekend.

2. Make sure that you keep boxes somewhere that you can get them out fast, in case it rains. You will want to have all of your items out of the boxes and priced before your sale starts, but lay out items so that you can easily put them back into a box in a hurry.

3. Get some waterproof tarps lined up before your sale. The bigger the tarps, the better. You can also use the tarps to cover your items after each day, so you don't get rain, dew, or dust on your items.

4. You have a lot more flexibility in how you organize tables, compared to a garage sale. Make sure that you give people room to pass each other comfortably in between the tables. You should set up your tables so that there is a flow to your sale, and shoppers end up naturally at your pay table.

5. I've been to a ton of sales that look like a bomb went off in the hosts' yard. Make your sale look neat, and people will feel more comfortable buying stuff from you.

6. Assign one host to be the organizer. She can keep your items looking good, which will directly need to more sales! Keep moving

items to the fronts of the tables as stuff sells. You don't want large open spaces on your tables. Eventually, you will want to remove tables when they start looking thin. The organizer can also make sure that price stickers are visible, toys are not where people can trip on them, and even perhaps make a run for drinks and food!

7. Chances are, you and your potential customers are going to be in the hot sun. Schedule your sale when it is not going to be 100 degrees. June is better than August in the US.

8. You can make some quick money by selling coffee when it is cool, or lemonade when it is hot. Better yet, have the kids do it!

9. I like having the toys table or area at the front of the sale, and off to the side. That way, your customers' kids are quickly satisfied, and they will often grab toys at the front of your sale just to shut the kids up, so they can shop. It also contains the mess off to the side, and keeps the rowdy kids from your book shoppers, who are often older adults.

10. For summer sales, start early. You will have early birds there before 7AM anyway, so start at 7. It is likely to be cool in the morning, and many people like to get things done in the summer while it is still tolerable. Research has shown that sales often slow considerably after noon. I like the 7-3 time slot for summer sales.

CONCLUSION

The proceeds from this document are dedicated to our children's college funds. I greatly appreciate your interest in my product. Please recommend this book to your friends and family. If you have a couple of minutes, please take the time to leave me five star feedback on Amazon by clicking on: http://www.amazon.com/dp/B00HUCT90S. Make sure that you continue and read the last couple of pages, which contain some excellent links to websites that you should visit for even more tips.

Good luck in your future endeavors, Eric Michael.

I would like to invite you to brag about your treasures found and partake in discussions about garage sailing and re-selling at the Almost Free Money Facebook http://www.facebook.com/almostfreemoney

and Garage Sale Academy Facebook http://www.facebook.com/garagesaleacademy pages.

WEBSITES AND LINKS

Here are some very helpful websites and web pages to jump start your research. These are my favorites, after completing many hours of surfing (You are welcome!)

1. Garage Sale Academy

http://www.garagesaleacademy.com

Our website has a ton of information about how to become a garage sale picker, and how to resell your garage sale finds on the internet. It expands the information from Almost Free Money by adding an entire niche on garage sale picking / shopping, and tons of information on how to get the best deals at sale, and find the best swag. It also has another niche for increasing the productivity of garage sales, yard sales, and estate sales for sale hosts. Garage Sale Academy also has links to the rest of the books in the Almost Free Money series, a garage sale forum, and a garage sale blog.

2. Its Deductible

https://itsdeductibleonline.intuit.com

As discussed in Donations section. Provides IRS-accepted values for your donations, and keeps track of your donations for the entire tax year. Inserts your donations into online Income Tax forms such as TurboTax.

www.ingramcontent.com/pod-product-compliance
Lightning Source LLC
Chambersburg PA
CBHW051639170526
45167CB00001B/249